Follow the Money

A Muslim Guide to the Murky World of Finance

FOLLOW
THE MONEY

A Muslim Guide to the Murky World of Finance

by
Abdassamad Clarke

DIWAN PRESS

Classical and Contemporary Books on Islam and Sufism

Copyright © Abdassamad Clarke

Published Muharram 1436/November 2014 by:
Diwan Press
6 Terrace Walk
Norwich
NR1 3JD
UK
website: http://www.diwanpress.com
email: info@diwanpress.com

By: Abdassamad Clarke
General Editor: Abdalhaqq Bewley

British Library Cataloguing in Publication Data
Clarke, Abdassamad

Follow the Money – A Muslim Guide to the Murky World of Finance
I. Title

ISBN 978-1-908892-44-7

Typeset by: Abdassamad Clarke
website: www.bogvaerker.dk
email: bookwright@bogvaerker.dk

Printed and bound by: Lightning Source

Contents

Acknowledgements

None of this would have been possible without the discovery by Shaykh Dr. Abdalqadir as-Sufi of the significance of this theme and his indefatigable work in single-handedly drawing attention to it over the years.

My thanks also to Shaykh Umar Vadillo for his tireless efforts in researching this matter, teaching it and striving to bring wholesome institutions and modalities into being.

I gratefully acknowledge the help of Dr. Riyad Asvat and Dr. Adi Setia, and the encouragement of Shaykh Ali Laraki. Particular thanks must go to Mahdi Lock whose carefully reading of the text and many corrections and suggestions have greatly improved the work. Many thanks to my wife Suád Østergaard for her painstaking reading of the book and for many helpful suggestions.

Introduction

Some people work all their lives for it. Some people have huge amounts of it, and some have almost none. Some steal it, some kill for it. Some men and women marry for it. Some people gamble everything they can, hoping to win more of it and some actually do win, but most lose. Some lie for it, some die for it. Many nations go to war for it. Most of the films we see and a great many of the stories we read are about people who do many of the above things for it. But what is money?

I am not going to try and answer this question with the help of famous economists. You will not find Adam Smith mentioned. Nor will you find Marx, Ricardo, or Milton Friedman. We will not talk a lot about inflation, gross national product or index-linked bonds. We will miss out many things that are supposed to go into a book on economics. We will also miss out many things that people now think ought to go into a book on 'Islamic Economics'. However, we will write many things that economists and 'Islamic' economists do not talk about and which you really ought to know. If that disappoints you, this is not the book for you. Otherwise, read on.

The Community and Age We're In

The modern world is a complex place. Ideologies and religions swirl, entangle with and wage war upon each other. Politically, socially and militarily the world is in upheaval. Economics, commerce and finance move in their own fashion and move many other forces from behind. The whole makes a strangely compelling but disturbing fabric of interwoven threads. And when was it ever different?

What the Muslim always brings to this intricate mix of good and bad is the knowledge that all of it proceeds from the Divine decree: NATO, burgeoning US hegemony, Russian counter moves or quiet Chinese expansion, just as much as the Crusaders and the Mongol hordes. Whatever the Muslim scans of history, biography, culture and technology, he is looking for the hand of Allah in that.

When he comes to act, then he knows that the intellect is a good servant but a bad master, as is evidenced by the whole epoch beginning with the Enlightenment and extending right up to our day. Thus, he turns to the Prophetic example for guidance, yet without abandoning his intellect but rather with it seeking to understand the revelation. The Arabic word for the science of the shari'a, **fiqh**, actually means 'understanding' rather than a ready-made bundle of laws imposed on the human situation.

As to the complex world of cause and effect, I have written this work in the conviction that the old journalist's rule "Follow the money" makes a lot of sense. Nevertheless, it is far from a book on economics.

As a Muslim author, it would be all too easy to tack on Islam at the end as 'the solution'. This present chapter is rather written in the conviction that an understanding of the mu'amalat or 'ordinary transactions' of the shari'a provides a grid that can be laid on economics that will illuminate it just as the Islamic era provides a suitable demarcation of the age we are in, the age that began with Muhammad, may Allah bless him and grant him peace. An Umma or community began then. The Arabic word 'Umma' denotes both a body of people and a time or epoch. It has two aspects: those who are invited to Islam and those who have accepted that invitation. But all are the Umma or community of Muhammad, peace be upon him.

Early trade and Quraysh

One small sura of Qur'an provides the first clue. Sura Quraysh is about the eponymous tribe among whom the Prophet Muhammad, peace be upon him, was born. The sura refers to the summer and winter caravans. Precariously lodged in a small town in the midst of the most arid desert, Quraysh embarked on winter trade caravans south to the Yemen and summer caravans north to Syria and Persia.

Yemenis were world class sailors of old, bringing goods from as far afield as India and China. This role of theirs lasted right up into the modern age, with the Yemenis bringing a very different trade: they were to take Islam to the entire east coast of Africa, Kerala on the west coast of India, Bengal and Nusantara — present day Indonesia and Malaysia. But they did that along with their trade. Reportedly it was their upright character in trade that proved the most effective means of calling people to Islam. The trader who has integrity and who remembers the Divine in the midst of the world and the marketplace is a rarity. Perhaps it is for that reason the Prophet, peace be upon him, said: "The truthful trustworthy trader will be with the prophets, the utterly truthful and the martyrs." (At-Tirmidhi, al-Hakim narrating from Abu Sa'eed) How different the modern world would be if the young men who choose haram suicide bombing as a route to martyrdom were to choose instead halal trade with integrity.

Quraysh's winter caravan brought them into contact with goods from India and China and the Far East. Most probably it also brought them into contact with some of their peoples.

Quraysh's summer caravan went north to Syria and Persia. The Eastern Roman Empire in Syria was a half of an empire whose western half reached up to the borders of Scotland. Roman citizens moved freely across the length and breadth of the Empire even after it divided into East and West. So Quraysh would almost certainly have rubbed shoulders with or traded with Europeans in the Syrian markets. But their goods would have been traded all the way to the North, as well as down to the South. Thus trade united what culture, religion, politics and war divided. They were at the centre of a trade crossroads that connected the Far East and the West.

Among the flow of all the goods was the money that expedited the trade: Roman denarius silver coins, and Greek silver drachmas. They were to give us units of weight: the dinar and the dirham. Later, gold and silver coins of those weights would be minted by Muslims.

Thus if someone trades in the gold and silver coins that are to hand, he has the precedent of his Prophet, peace be upon him. And if someone trades with specific gold dinars and silver dirhams, he has the precedent of 'Umar, who defined them from his tremendous knowledge of the way of the Prophet, and of 'Abdalmalik ibn Marwan, who minted them.

Quraysh was the tribe that the Prophet Muhammad, peace be upon him, was born into. This was the life he was born into. He was to train as a trader under his uncle, travelling on the caravans. Later he would marry Khadija, a wealthy merchant and manage her trade. This destiny, as with everything else about him, peace be upon him, was far from accidental. How could it be accidental, when nothing in existence is? But this one destiny was to have profound impact, not just on the Muslim community but on the world.

The beginning of Islam

Later the second khalifa 'Umar set about initiating a system of dating. Previously, years had been remembered by important things that had happened in them. Thus the year of the birth of the Prophet, peace be upon him, was also remembered as the Year of the Elephant because of the army from Yemen that had come with its elephant to attack Makka.

'Umar took counsel of all of the Companions. Some thought to date Islam from the birth or the death of the Prophet, may Allah bless him and grant him peace. Others suggested the date of the first revelation of the Qur'an. It was 'Ali ibn Abi Talib who suggested that the proper beginning was the emigration from Makka to Madina. That is when a living community had been founded on the basis of the revelation that had so long been denied in Makka. The Companions agreed on that unanimously. Islam began in Madina with the foundation of the community.

Just trade

That the background in trade is not accidental is underscored by a number of things that happened immediately after the emigration to Madina. The first sura of the Qur'an to be revealed in Madina was called The Stinters (al-Mutaffifin). It began with these words: **"Woe to the stinters, those who, when they take a measure from people, exact full measure, but when they give them a measure or weight, hand over less than is due."** (83:1-3) Until that moment, the Madinans had thought that Islam consisted of prayer and other religious acts but did not extend to behaviour in the market place. In other words, they thought that Islam was a religion. The first revelation in Madina disabused them of this notion. The issue here was disparity in weights and measures. Careful reflection will show that this all-encompassing prohibition also covers usury, because its essence is disparity.

One notable result of this revelation endures right down to today: very often when a Muslim trader weighs or measures out for a customer he will add something extra to ensure that he does not fit the description of the sura.

The free market

Famously, among the first actions of the Messenger of Allah, peace be upon him, was to found the mosque. It is less well known that at exactly the same time he established the market of Madina and established its ground rules. Those rules became the rules of all Muslim markets that were established thereafter.

> Abu Usayd said that a man came to the Prophet, may Allah bless him and grant him peace, and said, "May my father and my mother be your ransom! I have seen a place for the market; will you not then look at it?" He said, "Certainly." So he stood up and went with him until he came to the place for the market, and when he saw it he liked it and he stamped on it with his foot and said, "Your market is blessed, so let it not be broken up and let no tax be levied on it." (At-Tabarani)

> Muhammad ibn 'Abdullah ibn Hasan said, "The Messenger of Allah, peace be upon him, gave the Muslims their markets as a sadaqa." Meaning that they are free and that no rent can be charged on them. 'Umar ibn 'Abd al-'Aziz was a later khalifa of the Muslims. In conformity with this judgement he ordered that no rents could be charged for space in the marketplace.

This is a profound measure. The market is established as a free space which no one can reserve. Traders have to come early in the morning of each day and establish their stalls. No rent can be charged on it. "...let no tax be levied on it." No taxes are allowed to be charged on trade in the market. In other words, VAT — value added tax — is not permissible in Islam. It is, however, permissible for those responsible for maintenance of the market to charge some small fee for its upkeep. But the state may not levy a charge on trade.

Because trade is the lifeblood of civilisation, these generous trade-friendly ground-rules were established.

And this was right at the very beginning of Islam, i.e. right after the emigration to Madina and the establishment of a polity in accord with the Divine revelation. These are two of the fundamental matters relating to trade that were established, right alongside the founding of the mosque for the central pillar of Islam, the salat. See the importance given to trade.

Prices in the free market

The Messenger of Allah, peace be upon him, was asked by the people of Madina to set market prices but he refused to do so, saying that "Allah, He is the Pure, the One Who causes expansion and contraction, the One Who sets prices" (Ahmad, Abu Dawud, at-Tirmidhi, Ibn Majah and others). To fix prices would be an injustice to the traders. Capitalists have misunderstood this refusal to interfere in the market as an endorsement of 'free-market' capitalism. But free-market capitalism is the opposite of free and has taken ownership of the market.

Market regulation

Although prices may not be set, the qadi can expel traders from the markets for selling too expensively or too cheaply. 'Umar, the second khalifa, said to one of the Companions, "Either you must raise your price or you will be ejected from our market." (Muwatta, no. 1905) This is surprising to us. What possible harm could there be in selling cheaply? This, however, is the terrible practice of undercutting. Traders reduce the price to take trade from their brethren and to drive them out of business. The corporate world destroys traditional crafts and professions right across the earth precisely by this mechanism.

Equally, taking advantage of shortages by raising prices is scandalously immoral behaviour. What is the equitable resolution of these two matters, that prices may not be set by the ruler or the judge and that traders may be ejected from the market for selling too cheaply or too expensively? The judge must consult the traders in the market about the

7

real values of things. If they agree that someone's prices are too cheap or too expensive he can be asked to adjust his prices and if he does not then he is ejected. Thus the free market of Islam, unlike contemporary 'free-market' capitalism, places restrictions on the traders. It does not allow them total freedom to do what they wish inside the market place.

Usury

We have seen how trade provides the backdrop for the early years of the Prophet, peace be upon him. We have also seen what concern the very earliest revelations in Madina showed for trade and the market. Equally, this is underlined at the end by the prohibition of usury, which was the last of the shari'a to be revealed: **"But Allah has permitted trade and He has forbidden riba"** (2:275). Usury – riba – is defined linguistically as 'increase' or 'disparity'. That means extra in the exchange of quantities of gold, silver, or particular foodstuffs that are weighed or measured. Almost all modern banking and finance transactions are based on increase in the exchange for some and loss for others.

But ayat 281 in Surat al-Baqara shares something with the ayats on usury because some scholars also say that it is the very last ayat to be revealed. It is the longest ayat in the Qur'an. It is about debt, or you might say 'credit', since one man's debt is another's credit.

While this ayat does govern personal debts, the cause of the original revelation and its real significance relate to advancing credit commercially. That means it regulates delayed payment for goods that have already been delivered or, conversely, allowing for payment in advance for goods to be delivered later. These two uses are the lifeblood of trade and have been so throughout history. Such credit transactions in trade outweigh cash payments considerably. Credit is permissible when no charge is made for it.

Fascinatingly, the context was that the people of Madina made payment in advance for future crops. But this was not the establishment of a 'futures market' in which crops are sold repeatedly before they have been planted. Rather, when someone pays in advance for a crop he cannot resell it until he has taken possession of the crop itself, thus preventing the kind of speculative futures market that today artificially drives prices ever higher, making the prices of basic food commodities unreachable for poor people.

Trade and profit

Profit is not the same as disparity. Trade is not the same as usury. **"Allah has permitted trade and He has forbidden usury."** (Surat al-Baqara 2:275) There are numerous ways for people who are industrious or entrepreneurial to earn profit including qirad profit-sharing investment in trade or in acting as agents in wakala transactions or in seeking a markup on one's price for work done or for transporting the goods from city and city.

Trade was attended to at the beginning and at the end of the revelation. In between, many things were dealt with. That was either through revelation or through the behaviour or command of the Messenger of Allah, peace be upon him. No other revealed life-transaction has anything even remotely equivalent to this body of material. The **Muwatta** of Imam Malik, which records the practice of the first generations in Madina itself, has an extensive section on these types of issues. In another representative work, the **Mudawwana** of Sahnun from the same Madinan tradition, one quarter of the book is devoted to acts of worship and three-quarters to daily everyday matters such as marriage and divorce, and all the issues of buying, selling, renting, hiring, pledging, taking loans, credit and debt. Similar works can be found in all the major legal schools of Islam.

This material was absorbed by the Muslims both individually and as a community. As individuals it is incumbent on Muslims to know the rulings governing transactions. The second khalifa 'Umar said, "No one trades in our market except those who know fiqh". Fiqh is the science governing behaviour. What 'Umar meant was that we must know the laws governing behaviour in the market. As a community, it is incumbent on the Muslim leader to appoint a qadi or judge who is knowledgeable in these matters to arbitrate between people in their disputes. He in turn must appoint a market regulator, a muhtasib, who attends to checking the markets for its weights and measures and to prevent usury and other forbidden practices creeping in.

The actual texture of Muslims' civilisation was of a commercial trading culture. And, as we already mentioned, trade connects what race, politics, language, culture and religion divide. Everyone goes into the marketplace.

Now that may sound strange, because the reputation of Islam is for jihad. War.

In order to understand jihad, we need some context. The epoch prior to Islam was dominated by Roman power whose source was naked military might. The Romans unapologetically conquered. In their eastward progress they came up against the Persians. Their contest was to transform Persian society into a highly militarised and centralised empire like the Roman Empire. The Muslims took up arms against these two forces in that first memorable epoch of jihad. There was simply no possibility that either of them would leave the Muslims alone. After that first military expansion, Muslim civilisation took on its innate character of a cosmopolitan trading culture. This ethos was to affect the world and was to be one of the things transmitted to the West through the Crusades and the Renaissance. Fatally, Europe took that transmission without the checks and balances that prevented capitalism becoming the monster it has become today.

World Trade

W e have seen the fundamental part that trade played in the pre-Islamic setting in which the Prophet, peace be upon him, grew up, and in the process of the Qur'anic revelation of legal rulings itself. A few snippets will show us the continuing power that trade has and the influence it has exerted over world history.

Traffic along the nexus of routes known collectively as the Silk Road long predates Christianity. It tied together a number of great civilisations including India and China, and then later, with the advance of the Muslims, Arabia, Persia and Turkey.

A great interregnum in world history arguably begins from the moment when the Mongols swept away the Abbasid Khalifate and destroyed Baghdad in 1258. Surprisingly, this did not disrupt the trade of the Silk Road. This interregnum continued up until and after the fall of Constantinople to Mehmet al-Fatih in 1453 and the fall of Granada to Ferdinand and Isabella in 1492. It was in that latter year that Columbus obtained his commission from the two Spanish monarchs to sail West to reach the East, which he was never destined to see. What he and subsequent explorers were to find were the vast amounts of gold and silver that the Americas had. That was good news for a currency starved Europe but bad news for the native peoples of the Americas. He had set sail to open up the trade routes to the east since that was so important for Europe. Columbus's journey did not achieve that but a voyage undertaken for the same reason a few years later in 1497-1499 did. Vasco da Gama went East by travelling south, around the Cape of

Good Hope and then East. He reached India and the Indies.

His voyage signalled the demise of the Silk Road. The stock exchange in Venice collapsed at the news. Venice was the last call in Europe for the fabled Road. The Silk Routes had also brought vital revenue for all the lands through which they passed. These lands were largely Muslim and increasingly a part of the expanding Osmanlı (Ottoman) domains. The combined effect of floods of South American gold and silver into Europe and new trade routes for European merchants that bypassed Asia were to deal a disastrous blow to the Osmanlı civilisation at precisely its zenith. A century later, another force would make use of these new trade routes to devastating effect.

The British East India Company

Nothing illustrates so perfectly the power of trade and its centrality to the movement of history as the history of the East India Company. The Company was only one of several European East India companies competing for the lucrative trade of the east in fabrics and spices. The rise of Europe at this time was through its adventurous traders, who, being seafaring folk, had as much pirate in them as merchant. Founded in 1600 with a Royal Charter from Elizabeth I, the Company started trading in the Indies, but came to focus on India. There it founded the cities that were to become Madras, Calcutta and Bombay, establishing factories for the manufacture of the cotton goods that were so much in demand in Europe.

Dealing in things such as Indian textiles and spices, the company prospered. Soon it founded armies to secure its properties and guard its trade. It came to deal on equal terms with local rulers and with the Mughal Emperor. Finally its armies defeated its competitors from other nations as well as the Mughals themselves and in 1757 the Company was left as de facto ruler of India. That endured for a century until 1857 when the 'Indian Mutiny' of the Muslim and Hindu Sepoy soldiers against the Company broke out. In the next year, the British Government stepped in and assumed control of India. Queen Victoria was crowned Empress of India and the British Empire became a fact. It had been brought into existence by a Company.

Yet at the heart of the entire venture lurked a fatal sickness. Since the European ethos of trade lacked discrimination, there was no protection against usury. Europe was entering what it considered the Enlightenment, which took a 'scientific' stance. Traditional perspectives on usury were viewed askance. The English philosopher Bentham wrote a book called "In Defence of Usury". Banking and finance established themselves at the heart of the new trade. But where usury finance goes, credit swells exorbitantly as does debt, and financiers swallow the proceedings.

British decline was brought about by a single war that has been called the European Civil War of 1914-1945 or the Second Thirty Years War, but which most people call the First and Second World Wars. This bankrupted Britain, which had started the Second World War as the largest empire the world had ever seen but by the end of it had to wind the Empire up. This marked the end of a mode of trade that had endured for millennia but which had increasingly become swallowed up by the cancer of finance.

Barter

The oldest form of trade is barter. That means to exchange one item for another. For example, you might exchange an axe for a spear, or a DVD for a book.

People say that it soon becomes inconvenient to exchange things. Perhaps the two parties do not really have things that the other wants or only one of them has something the other wants. You might want a friend's book and he might be willing to exchange it, but you might not have anything he wants. That is true. People invented the idea of money to solve that problem. That is not completely true.

If you look closely, you will see that using money is really another type of barter, or used to be. People discovered gold and silver, and other things which are valuable to them. It was found that it was almost always possible to barter gold and silver for anything. It became so useful that it led to the minting of coins about 2,500 years ago.

The idea behind barter is simple. It is when both people in the deal are equally pleased with the thing they receive in exchange for the thing they have given. It is good for both of them. Allah mentions that in an ayat of Qur'an *"***an taraadin minkum** — by means of mutually agreed trade" (Surat an-Nisa' 4:29) or actually: mutually pleasing trade. It is symbolised by the ancient image of the scales which are used to weigh things. When the two pans of the scales are equal and level, then the deal can be done. This is the symbol of barter, and it is the universal symbol of justice.

Real trade is like that. Both parties are pleased with what they get. Indeed, they both make a profit out of it. It is not as some economists try to paint it saying that life and the market are "survival of the fittest", "dog eat dog" and "the law of the jungle." That is not true of nature and it is not true of most people. It certainly is true of many of the top capitalists and bankers because that is how they behave. It is not how life really is.

Allah's generosity is the reality of existence. It is possible for two people to trade with each other and for both to make a profit from it. They can both be pleased with it and they do not need to trick and deceive each other.

Using money was originally just one type of barter. There is a still a great deal of barter going on in our shops and markets and homes. It has been said that even today a fifth of all world trade is still barter. Sophisticated economies exchange oil for chemicals, and food for aeroplanes.

That means that we do not need to be stuck with one 'money', even gold or silver. Anything can be money if both parties are happy with it, but let us look at the most popular money in all history: gold and silver coins. Let us look at the coins the Muslims used throughout history: the dinar and the dirham.

What is money?

We think we already know the answer to this. Whether we are seven or seventy years old, everyday we give people something we call money and they give us things in exchange: bus tickets, things to eat, or mobile phones.

The conventional answer to the question is that long ago people used to exchange things in a system called 'barter', but that they found it was much simpler to trade once a medium of exchange had been invented, and that people have used salt, sea-shells and many other things as money. All of this we will look at later in the book, but for now let us look quickly at today's money.

Types of money
There is little, medium and big money.

The Little Money
The little money is made of metal. Some of it is often goldish looking and some silverish. Of course, the small coins are not gold and silver. But why do I say, 'Of course'? Until recently many coins were made only of gold or silver. Now they are not. There is a third one which looks like copper and sometimes actually is copper. A paradox of the time is that often copper coins were entirely symbolic and their value was simply set by custom but that today they often have value simply by their copper content and sometimes are even more valuable for that than their face value would suggest.

The Medium Money

The medium pieces of money are made of paper, most of the time at least — the dollar is made of cotton and linen and some bank notes are even made of plastic. However for convenience, and historical reasons we'll talk about later, we refer to all of the above as paper money. There is a lot of writing and different designs on the paper. Some of them are quite pretty, or they would be if they didn't crumble and become dirty so quickly.

On some of the British paper notes there are strange messages such as "I promise to pay the bearer on demand the sum of five pounds." It is signed by the Governor of the Bank of England.

There are few people who know what this statement really means. For example, is one supposed to go and find the Governor of the Bank of England 'bearing' the piece of paper money? Will he then give you another five pound note as well as the one you have, just because you went to all the trouble of looking for him? Is it some strange kind of competition that nobody knows about? Or will he just change the one that you give him for another one? Perhaps he will give you a brand new one instead of the crumpled one. It really is a puzzle.

This small and medium sized money is now only a tiny part of all the money that people use. Some say that in Britain, for example, it is only around 3% of all money!

The Big Money

What about the rest of the money? That is in the form of cheques, credit cards and many other things. We will find that we have come into a strange world indeed, in this world of money, and cheques and credit cards are some of the strangest bits in that world . We will delay looking at them until later.

Where does money come from?

Paper money and coins

In England, paper money is printed by De La Rue Currency under the auspices of the Bank of England and coins are minted by the Royal Mint. In America it comes out of the US Treasury, the coins through the Bureau of the Mint and the paper notes through the Bureau of Engraving and Printing. They are then sold to the Federal Reserve bank. The paper money is sold at the cost of printing, and the coins at face value.

In America it costs approximately 4 cents to print a $1 note. Presumably, it also costs about 4 cents to print a $100 note. The people who print these notes pay 4 cents and for little expense they get lots of dollars. That is a good business.

State fiat money

However that already quite strange picture only represents approximately 3% of all money, the small change. Most money has an even odder origin. It comes into existence by **fiat** — i.e. the command 'let it exist'. It is **fiat money.** The dollar only exists at the very instant when the Federal Reserve uses it for the purchase of treasury bonds from the US Treasury. Those bonds represent this: "We the US Government would like to borrow such-and-such a sum of money. We promise to repay it with interest and for that repayment and interest we will tax the population of the USA." So the Federal Reserve are allowed to invent money in order to buy bonds from the government guaranteeing them to receive compensation from the taxes of ordinary people.

You can understand why other people want to get into that business. Some people use colour printers to make their own money. We are not saying that they are right to do that, but that the people who control banks are wrong to do what they are doing. They are also forging money. But people who make most of the money in existence (although most of it does not 'exist' in any tangible sense) do so simply by typing numbers on a keyboard! What on Earth can we say about them?

It is, however, actually legal in many countries, including Britain, to use gold and silver coins to buy and sell, even though they are not 'legal tender'. Legal tender is the kind of thing that you can pay your bills with: rent, gas, electricity and phone. It is what you can use without thinking about it for shopping. For legal tender we must use credit cards, paper money and the coins that everyone uses. To do that we are supposed to have jobs and earn money, or start businesses. If people want more money than they can earn in those ways, they have to go to the bank and ask them politely if they can have some. People then must agree to pay extra for the use of the bank's dollars or pounds.

Let us take a look at one of the institutions that make money.

The Bank of Sweden

In 1657 the Swedish king, Charles X Gustav, permitted the foundation of Stockholms Banco and in 1661 allowed it to print banknotes called **Kreditivsedlar**, literally: "credit notes". Sweden had wrestled with currency issues for a long time, having little gold and silver of its own. The result had been a period in which they issued heavy copper coins whose face value was the value of the weight of copper. With the foundation of the new bank, Johan Palmstruch, the banker, could not resist the urge to print a great many banknotes, with predictable consequences: galloping inflation and a crash. It was an ominous note, warning of what was to follow. The bank ceased operations in 1664.

The Bank of England

The Bank of England was founded in 1694 and issued its first paper money in 1696.

Everybody in Europe had used gold and silver coins to pay each other. Why then did the English create the Bank of England? Why did they make those first banknotes? The reason: there was a war.

The merchants and businessmen had become important in Britain. They began to turn from the real business of trade to earning money with their money; they would become the new bankers and their wealth would begin its exponential growth. They kicked out the old British king, James the Second, and invited in a new king from Holland, William of Orange, James's son-in-law. The people didn't really like that and felt that the old king was the rightful king, and that they couldn't just kick him out because they didn't like him.

James went to France where the French king gave him some support. He wanted an army to return and fight William. William too had to raise an army. Armies cost money, lots of money. When they had insufficient funds, kings used to borrow money from someone, pay for the war, win the battles if they could and then tax everybody to pay back the loan. In Europe that loan usually involved interest.

But William had a problem. If he taxed everybody to pay for this army and this war, he would have to increase taxes a great deal. People already did not like him. If he taxed them more than they were already taxed, they would like him even less and perhaps fight against him.

William's problem was also a problem for the businessmen who had invited him to come. If he was defeated they would be in trouble, and so they came up with a plan. Note, this was a plan not a conspiracy.

The national debt

That plan resulted in the Bank of England and the National Debt.

Neither a national bank nor a national debt had ever been seen or heard of before. There had been bankers before, in Italy, Germany and Holland, but their banks were not national banks. Kings had debts before with interest charged on the loan, but they paid them off.

The deal was that the businessmen lent William £1,200,000 in real money: gold and silver, not paper money. They charged him 6% interest per year on the loan, but the intention was that he would never repay the loan. If William had to repay the loan, as we saw, he would have had to put taxes up too much in order to repay more than a million pounds. Remember that was an enormous sum of money at that time.

With just a small increase in taxes, he could pay 6% every year without too much bother. After some years he had repaid much more money than the original debt, but that was concealed. It is similar to the situation when people today buy houses through mortgages. In some countries they are paying as much as three times the price of their house. Because they do that over many years, even their whole lives, it doesn't seem so much to them. Perhaps that is why it is called a 'mort-gage' — 'a death pledge'.

William's not repaying the loan was a part of their plan. Who would be responsible for the debt? The nation became responsible and so it is called the National Debt. It was the first ever in history. This is one of the key moments in the creation of the modern state. Not the king but the nation, through its elected representatives, are responsible for the national debt. Very quickly the debt grew to be much larger than that £1,200,000. Now[1] it is approximately £1.2 trillion, i.e. £1,200,000,000,000. In other words, a million times larger.

Paper money
That wasn't all of their plan. The businessmen knew that William wasn't in a position to make bargains. They got as much out of him as they could. In addition, the businessmen negotiated the right to make

1   Late 2013. One has to date such statistics since they change so quickly.

paper money. They were allowed to make exactly the same amount of paper money – £1,200,000 – as they had lent the king. That money was lent out to people at exactly the same rate of interest, 6%. The same sum of money was lent out twice and interest charged for it both times.

This strange behaviour is now regular practice. Whenever a government takes a loan from the banking system, the banks call it an 'asset'. They then lend the same amount of money to people at interest. I told you that this would be a strange story.

At first this paper money was not printed. Clerks wrote out the banknotes and the Governor of the Bank signed each one by hand. A few years later, they printed all the notes but the Governor still signed each one.

Now, this is a book by a Muslim published by an Islamic publishing company whose books are largely read by Muslims or people drawn to or interested in Islam. You might well ask why I am writing this book. It is because every country in the world, including every single Muslim country, has followed the same road as these people did. Every country now has a national bank, a national paper currency, a national debt and enormous taxation. It is interesting for us to see how it all started.

We are so used to money and banks that we almost assume that they were always there. But the Native American peoples and the Celts didn't have banks, nor did they have paper money. Neither did the Arabs nor the people of the sub-continent of India. Neither did the Messenger of Allah, may Allah bless him and grant him peace, establish a national debt, massive loans at interest, or paper money.

An admission from the Bank of England
As I worked on the final draft of this book, the Bank of England published an extraordinary document in its quarterly bulletin of March

2014.[2] It laid bare the actual mechanisms behind the creation of money today. Ordinarily this matter is only talked about by alternative economists or conspiracy theorists. The authors of this document wrote:

> Whenever a bank makes a loan, it simultaneously creates a matching deposit in the borrower's bank account, thereby creating new money.

> ...The reality of how money is created today differs from the description found in some economics textbooks:

> • Rather than banks receiving deposits when households save and then lending them out, bank lending creates deposits.

But more astonishing than that barefaced admission is that Alan Holmes, then Vice-President of the New York Federal Reserve, had already admitted the same thing in 1969, when he said, "In the real world, banks extend credit, creating deposits in the process, and look for the reserves later."[3]

Commercial banks actually 'create money out of nothing'. This earth-shaking fact can only pass largely unnoticed because of some extraordinary somnambulistic condition. Money today is **'fiat'** money. This is as in the Latin version of the Bible when God said **"fiat lux –** let there be light". Man does not have such divine powers. This act of creation by man is an act of magic, i.e. hypnotism. Hans Christian Andersen's "Emperor's New Clothes" has turned out to be true. The Emperor IS naked but we all pretend that he is fully clothed in the most beautiful suit he has ever worn.

But this danger has been warned against repeatedly. We take, almost

2   "Money creation in the modern economy" by Michael McLeay, Amar Radia and Ryland Thomas of the Bank's Monetary Analysis Directorate.
3   "Operational Constraints on the Stabilization of Money Supply Growth", http://www.bostonfed.org/economic/conf/conf1/conf1i.pdf

at random, one voice:

> "It had been justly stated by a British writer that the power to make a small piece of paper, not worth one cent, by the inscribing of a few names, to be worth a thousand dollars, was a power too high to be entrusted to the hands of mortal man." [John C. Calhoun, speech, U.S. Senate, Dec. 29, 1841] [4]

We must retrace our steps. Where did all this come from? Obviously banks weren't always there. Let us go a little further back in European history.

---

4   http://etymonline.com/index.php?allowed_in_frame=0&search=money&searchmode=none

Mess with money at your peril

Money has two dynamics: to take and to give. Most transactions consist of taking and giving by both parties. Taking involves earning, inheriting and acquiring by other means including theft, usury, and plunder in wartime. Giving includes gifts and charity. When taking dominates giving certain results ensue.

First step, permit a small sect of usurers to provide loans and to charge the execrated usury, and bit by bit money – gold and silver – gravitate into their vaults. A new principle is unleashed: increase. Without any effort the wealth of a few increases, and, in spite of their best efforts, the wealth of many people decreases dramatically and they move quickly into the zone of accelerating negative equity – debt. A new mathematics is discovered: exponential growth. It applies both in gain and loss. Mathematicians found exponential growth when exploring the workings of interest.

Second step, others compete with the original outsider usurers since the principle is so simple and so enriching for some – and the race accelerates. Gold and silver all but vanish and are replaced by paper, and later naked digits. The newly engorged wealthy élite discover the Maecenas complex of 'philanthropy', part guilt, part sheer relish at seeing others cower and crawl before their wealth. Nevertheless, from these people came art, culture, science, philosophy, technology and more. We enter the Renaissance.

Third step, the paper and digits can be inflated beyond measure, but the result is, naturally enough, inflation. Values perpetually sink and prices rise. In the short term, crisis. In the long term, gradual but inexorable devaluation of the currency.

Fourth step, foreclosure on landowners who unwisely took loans they could never repay (no loan that keeps growing can ever be repaid, without plunder of some kind) and who pledged their land as surety.

Fifth step, force the land to yield profit rather than to sustain people. The Enclosures and Clearances. This epoch in history doesn't read well.

Sixth step, the people cleared from the land surge into the cities without gainful employment. Great poverty, great degradation. Poor women are forced into prostitution, which is not a moral issue but an economic one.

Seventh step, they become a 'workforce' in the 'labour market'.

Eighth step, since the money must grow, it must do some work in order to pay its way. Outlets must be found for it. A new type of industry is invented. Some carefully crafted shoes for the community will not do. There must be millions of shoes. At first they are all identical and not that well made. Later they can all be different. A plethora of styles and shapes.

Ninth step, when people are utterly defeated, coerced and humiliated they are allowed to become 'consumers' and indeed 'citizens'. They can even vote, although everyone knows that is a waste of time. For their pains, they are allowed to pay taxes. Roads are built, pavements paved, sewers provided, fresh water pumped in and purified, gradually electricity is wired to every house. Mass education swings into effect, mass medical treatment too.

Tenth step, among the items and besides the innocuous shoes, are the shiny new weapons. They also pour off the assembly line ready for the anxious masses who will do whatever is needed to earn the elusive money that puts food on the table, as they think. Among the uses of the weapons are to get the plunder that states need to pay the exponentially growing public debts. Wars become even more obviously devoted to plunder, although that is certainly not a modern invention. An industry grows to hide the naked anxiety and greed that drive the war machine and to tell another story: the media.

Eleventh step, no sane person will buy the new mass-produced shoddy goods when set beside a craftsman's work. A new economics is needed: undercutting. The price is lowered. The stressed consumer falls for it. Entire traditions of craft and skill go to the wall. Retailers go to the wall. That means independent livelihood goes to the wall. Independence itself is all but gone. Welcome corporate man.

Twelfth step, the goods pour out of the factories faster than anyone could possibly consume them. Life has to change. Either the shoes are so shoddy that you perpetually need new shoes (planned obsolescence), or the shoes perpetually change. Fashion is born. Style dies. People used to wear shoes because they had to live. People are now needed who will live in order to wear shoes.

Thirteenth step, money must be kept moving and growing and thus new lands and their inhabitants are needed. More people are required who will live to wear shoes rather than wearing shoes to live. The restless armies and the anxious masses of enlisted men and women come in handy too.

Fourteenth step, the ballooning wealth of the few grows beyond all bounds. The ballooning debts of the many outstrip them. Both have now outgrown the productivity of the entire planet many times over. 'Derivatives' are invented and they quickly dwarf the economy of the planet and look set to dwarf the galaxy.

If under the spell of a seemingly inexorable fate, people continue in thrall to the process it must go to end game. But, none of the steps are inevitable. People — individuals, families, communities and nations — can step out of the process at any point they wish. For that to happen, they must recognise the first step that took them to this end: taking dominated giving.

Let us go right back to the beginning and do justice to 'taking'. The Church 'took' tithes from the wealthy for the poor. The more the Church became enmeshed in usury, the less it guarded that function. Then we reach the age we are in. All that is left is a token Christian 'charity'. Even the Muslims are content with a token charity. Zakat has been redesigned to fit.

The way back is to go forward. We go back to the primal taking that was lost, the taking that corresponded to a selfless giving. But to do that we have to go on to the zakat, which must be taken.

Muslims' money

In the first days of Islam, the Muslims used whatever coins there were. The coins were the gold and silver ones that the Romans and Persians made.

A coin is not something magical. Really it is only a standard measure of gold or silver. The designs of coins or the writing on them are nothing to do with their value. It is the weights of gold and silver that determines their value.

The responsibility of a ruler has always been to see that the coin really is pure gold or silver and that it has the right weight. Muslims saw 90% as the minimum acceptable purity. Modern processes permit much greater values of 99% purity and more. When a ruler allows his name to be put on a coin, he is in effect saying, "This coin is so many carat of gold or silver, and it has such and such a weight and my officials have verified that."

Then people only need to count coins rather than having to weigh them and do a lot of calculations. But, in great trading cities of the world, there were often many kinds of coins from different places. Rulers minted all sorts and shapes and sizes of coins, therefore traders used to carry little sets of scales to weigh coins and sometimes there were specialists in the markets who could be relied on for this. In Arabic someone like that was known as a "**sayrafi**".

Rulers today do not bother to do any of these things. They allow their banks to handle all of it and thus money has become what it has.

If you look closely you can easily see that the ostensible rulers no longer have any real power. Banks and financial institutions have power. Kings, queens and presidents are only employed to look after ceremonies. Even presidents, prime ministers and other government officials do not have much power. Corporations and banks are much more important today than governments.

The history of coins

The Khalifa Umar ibn al-Khattab, may Allah be pleased with him, defined the weights. The system of weights and measures he defined according to his knowledge of the Sunna is something that all the Muslims have agreed about since the beginning of Islam and the age of the Companions and the Followers. Before being names for coins, the dinar and dirham were two units of weight. Ten dirhams weigh the same as seven **mithqals** of gold. A dinar is a mithqal. The weight of the dirham is seven-tenths of the weight of a dinar. There is another weight used for weighing silver called an **uqiya**. An **uqiya** is the weight of forty dirhams.

The Muslims used to weigh small things against grains of barley. Remember that Islam is the deen of **fitr**: Islam is the natural way. The kilogram is defined by scientists as a mass equal to that of a platinum-iridium cylinder which is held at the International Bureau of Weights and Measures at Sévres, France. This is an unnatural way but it is more 'scientific'.

Traditionally, people weighed and measured with things that they knew locally. They used to measure with the 'cubit' which is the measure from the finger-tips to the elbow. The 'foot' is of course the length of a foot. A 'span', which is used to measure the heights of horses, is the distance between the end of the thumb and the end of the little finger when the hand is fully extended. These measures are not exact, but they were good enough for what people needed.

In the scientific age, we weigh with artificial measures which are defined by scientists. That is so that they can measure tiny things like atoms and enormous things like galaxies, and so that the measurements will be identical in all parts of the cosmos whether the weather is hot or cold, whether people are tall or short, and in all circumstances. This view of existence was greatly undermined by Einstein's Special Theory of Relativity that showed that at great speeds our frames for measuring with are not as absolute as we had thought and weights and measures are not the absolutes we had thought.

But, remember that Islam too is a science, the science of living. Islam makes a healthy society with people who are fulfilled, and takes people to the Garden in the next life and not to the Fire. There are people who study physics, economics and sociology who say that they are scientists. They have invented a technology which is powerful, but their society is falling apart. Modern people are dreadfully lonely and unhappy. Which is the more important science?

That does not mean that we have to choose between these two types of science. It does mean that it is more important to begin with the science of life, rather than the science of machines. The people who have the science of life can also understand the science of machines. The people who have the science of machines can never understand the science of life because life is not a machine.

Using these traditional measures, the weight of a **mithqal** of gold is seventy-two grains of barley. The dirham is seven-tenths of a dinar in weight, and so the weight of the dirham is fifty and two-fifths grains. The Muslims have always agreed about these measurements.

The Khalifa Uthman, may Allah be pleased with him, was one of the first to mint coins, using the coins of the Persians and re-minting one face. Uthman used the coins that Yezdigird, the last ruler of the Persian Sassanian Empire, had made, the only difference being that on one side of the coin he ordered that "In the Name of Allah" be written.

In the year 75 AH (695 CE), the Khalifa Abdalmalik ordered al-

Hajjaj to mint the first completely original Islamic dirhams. He officially established the standard that Umar ibn al-Khattab had laid down from his knowledge of the Sunna and which is absolutely agreed upon.

> "Know that there is consensus since the beginning of Islam and the age of the Companions and the Followers that ten dirhams of the shari'a weigh seven mithqals weight of the dinar of gold... The weight of a mithqal of gold is seventy-two grains of barley, so that the dirham, which is seven-tenths of it, is fifty and two-fifths grains. All these measurements are firmly established by consensus." (Ibn Khaldun, al-Muqaddima)

The year after that he ordered dirhams to be minted in all the regions of Dar al-Islam. All the coins were stamped with the sentence: **"Allahu ahad. Allahu's-samad** – Allah is Absolute Oneness, Allah is the Everlasting Sustainer of all." Before Islam, people used to put animal figures and human faces on coins as they do in many countries today. Abdalmalik ordered the removal of human figures and animals and said they must be replaced with writing. This command of his has been obeyed throughout all the history of Islam.

Remember that 'the Sunna' also includes the Sunna of the Khulafa who took the right way after the Prophet, may Allah bless him and grant him peace. The best of all the Khulafa were the first four, Abu Bakr, Umar, Uthman and Ali, may Allah be pleased with them. Abdalmalik was also an important khalifa and when he minted the coins he established their Sunna. He was a khalifa at a time when many of the great Companions were still alive, from whom he had learnt and who either endorsed what he did or remained silent. Silence is also an endorsement, particularly from people who will not remain quiet in the face of falsehood.

The dinar and the dirham were both circular. The writing was stamped in concentric circles, with **"la ilaha illa'Allah** – there is no god but Allah" and **"al-hamdu lillah** – praise belongs to Allah" usually written on one side. On the other side the name of the amir who had ordered the coins minted and the date were written.

The amir's name was written because he was ultimately responsible for seeing that the weights of the coins were correct and that they were pure metals. Totally pure gold is usually too soft to make coins. So gold coins include a little extra silver and copper in order to strengthen them, up to a maximum of 10%. Modern techniques allow one to make coins that are much purer than that without them being too soft. Later on it became usual to include blessings on the Prophet, peace be upon him, and sometimes ayats of the Qur'an.

Gold and silver coins were official currency until the fall of the Khalifate. Gold and silver were used by the Muslims for more than 1,300 years. Human beings have used gold and silver coins for more than 2,500 years. No government told them to do that. They naturally found that they are the most suitable.

But banks and financiers have slowly come to own more and more of the gold. Instead of coins bankers have given people paper. That happened first in Europe and America. Since then, dozens of different paper currencies have been made in each of the new Muslim countries.

Flous

There is another coin which has been used by the Muslims since the earliest days. It was a coin which was called **flous** and was ordinarily made of copper or nickel. It was different from the gold and silver coins in an important way. The values of gold and silver coins are in their weights of gold and silver. The value of flous is only what is written on it. The value of flous is never more than half a dirham and it was used to buy small daily things like bread and vegetables, things which are cheap.

In the main, there is no zakat to be paid on flous, because it is not gold or silver. Some people say that one should find out its value if one has a great deal of it and pay the zakat on it in gold and silver along with one's zakat. One certainly ought not to pay zakat **with** flous, unless it impossible to pay with gold and silver.

When the colonialists came to Muslim lands with their paper money, the Muslims thought that it was flous. The history of European money and banking was not well known and so few knew that in those days paper money was an IOU. Now modern Arabs call modern paper money and the coins which are in everyday use 'flous'. It was thought that flous just means money, but this is not correct.

If paper money is flous, one does not pay zakat with it except in impossible situations. But, when paper and digital money were an IOU it was absolutely impossible to pay zakat with it. One really ought not to buy anything with it at all. That is because you cannot pay somebody with someone else's IOU. There are strict rules in shari'a for paying people with debts. Modern money is not even an IOU since it is invented from nothing and is 'fiat' money, as we saw.

When we say that zakat cannot be paid with paper and digital money, we are not criticising those Muslims who give some of their earnings away in charity in order to pay their zakat. But we are also sure that when they understand about the history and nature of such money, they will want to own dinars and dirhams in order to pay their zakat in the way of the Sunna.

The IOU

It used to be that you could really go into a bank and get gold and silver for your paper money. This is the secret of the phrase "I promise to pay the bearer on demand the sum of ..." that is still written on British notes, for example. Many years ago, redemption of paper notes in gold and silver was stopped, and now our money is an IOU that no one will ever pay. It is true that you can go out and buy gold and silver but that does not make up for the banks' broken promise to 'pay the bearer on demand.' See how this alteration in the nature of money affects people's lives.

The person who has a job with a wage or a salary is really paying something precious: the hours of his or her life, since most people are paid for the hours they work. Those hours are gone and can never come back again. The employers pay us with bits of paper or by crediting our bank accounts with numbers digitally. Those bits of paper tell us that someone will pay us real money if we want. Most of us do not know that is what it means or that we will never be paid with real money. Deep down inside we do not feel satisfied with those bits of paper or those digital bank entries in our accounts.

When we go shopping we take our credit and debit cards and these often dirty pieces of paper and exchange digits or paper for things: food, clothing, things for the home, and luxury items. In the age in which we live, people spend a lot. It is as if we know unconsciously that the real value of the money is not there, and we want to replace what we have lost of our lives by buying 'things'. On the other hand, people who use gold and silver to buy are often more careful about what they buy and want to hold on to the gold and the silver.

The danger for people who use gold and silver is meanness and miserliness. We don't want to let go of gold and silver because deep down we know that they have real value. But modern people have a different idea of money. We know deep in our hearts that today's money is not real. We try and get rid of it as soon as we can. We buy and sell in a different way from the way people used to.

Online and electronic purchases
There is one other matter we must deal with. Today people use credit cards and cheques a great deal. These are almost the strangest forms of money. We delayed looking at them to begin with but now we must examine them.

Whenever we write a cheque or pay for goods using our credit cards, we invent money. Sometimes the money that we invent actually corresponds to some that we have deposited in our accounts, but often today it does not. It is 'credit' and we have created it. 'Credit' comes from the Latin root 'credo' — 'I believe'. Originally it meant that others 'believed' that the debtor had assets sufficient to cover his debts or that his integrity in money matters was so reliable that they were sure to be repaid.

Today it means that we believe that we will get paid one day with something real, but we have seen that reality receding further away in this world of virtual money. There is an agreement with the bank or the credit card company that we can invent money which they don't have and for which we will pay the bank or credit card company interest.

There is another aspect of cheques and credit cards which is useful and which we cannot imagine living without. We can pay for things at some distances. We can order goods and services from other cities in our own countries or from the other sides of the earth and pay for them by these means. Particularly today, with the great ease of electronic communication, many private people and business people experience this as a necessity and not a luxury. If you told us that we could only use physical dinars and dirhams, we would feel that we had gone back in time.

Muslims always had facilities for dealing with these matters. Remember that the Muslim community spans from Malaysia to Morocco, and from Siberia to Cape Town. Indeed today there is almost nowhere left without a Muslim community. Muslim merchants travelled and traded incessantly. They devised means in accordance with the shari'a to move funds. On the basis of those means, there are ways which Muslims can use today that will rival credit cards, but not involve their haram aspects.

There are two main transactions involved in this, both of which are acceptable in the shari'a: first, that a Muslim should store our dinars and dirhams on our behalf in a safe place; second, that a Muslim should act as an agent (**wakeel**) for us and pay another person dinars and dirhams on our behalf. The first is a physical job of storing real gold dinars and silver dirhams in a safe place. The second can be done in a number of ways, but today it can also be done by electronic means and over the Internet. In this case, it means that the ownership of the coins which are stored is transferred to the other person; the coins themselves do not move, unless their owner asks to have them removed from safekeeping and sent to him.

The persons who store your coins and pay them to someone else on your behalf may not themselves lend them to anyone else. They may not send an electronic signal that claims that you or anybody else have coins in storage which you do not, or that you or anyone else are paying for something which you are not. It is obvious that fraud is possible and so there have to be some safeguards.

The third element that is needed is an independent body set up under the society's **qadi** (judge) which will check on the organisation to make sure that it has exactly the amount of precious metals in its vaults that its records show, and that its transactions are all correct. Thus, you can see that there is a possibility based on traditional Islamic fiqh for paying for things with dinars over distances and electronically.

The fourth element is the presence of political leadership that will enforce the judgement of the qadi, for, without that power, his judgements are useless. That is the issue that ceaselessly confronts the Muslims: the fact that so many things cannot be achieved without some authentic form of Muslim leadership with actual power. Here we are not talking about an Islamic state, but to examine this issue is a huge matter that is probably beyond the capacity of this book to approach let alone examine.

Other money that people use
Last of all, almost anything — except for paper and digital signals — can be money, if all the people involved are happy with it. That is also a part of the meaning of barter. Almost any commodity can be used: bags of wheat, cattle, un-minted gold and silver or whatever people agree is valuable and which they are mutually pleased with using in exchanges.

Bitcoin

We save perhaps the strangest of all money to the end. Bitcoin was born out of the hacker community and its resentment of and resistance to corporatism. It comprises two aspects: the 'coins' themselves and transactions involving them. Suffice it to say that this is simply the logical extension of the process we have followed whereby actual physical coins were substituted first by IOUs, then by fiat paper money, then increasingly by digital credit money. Although it is popularly seen as an 'alternative currency' it leads further down a path away from real wealth.

Where do banks come from?

There are many types of banks. The Bank of England, we have looked at above, is a national bank and it is owned by the nation, although it was a private bank, throughout its history, until just after the Second World War.

Other banks, including some 'national banks', are businesses making money for themselves and for their shareholders. Some, such as the N. M. Rothschilds bank in London, are private 'merchant' banks. That means that they do not have shareholders and so by law do not have to publish their accounts.

The Bank of England was actually a private bank for most of its history until after the Second World War when in 1946 it was nationalised. You might ask how a 'national' bank could have been 'private'. That would be a good question to ask.

The American Federal Reserve Banks and Federal Reserve System seem to be part of the American government. Most people think that they are American institutions rather than businesses like Microsoft or Coca Cola. Their true nature is somewhat complex but they are certainly much more than just government organs. Yet they are not entirely private bodies. They were founded officially in 1915 but in reality had been founded in 1910 on Jekyll Island at a private meeting of Rockefellers, Morgans, Warburgs and Rothschilds. It is this confluence of state and bank that would increasingly come to dominate the times to come. It is arguable that today the state is no longer capable of acting independently of banking.

In a few other countries, such as Scotland and Northern Ireland, many private banks print their own banknotes. Those banks are not owned by the state. If you then take that money abroad and try to change it in a German bank, for example, you can waste a lot of time as they try to find out what on earth this money is. Usually, however, it is central banks or similar institutions that are responsible for printing and minting the money. Banks have only come about in recent centuries. They have a number of different origins: the goldsmith, the merchant and the scrivener, i.e. the writer who recorded loan contracts.

The goldsmith

Before the rise of banking the only people in cities and towns who had safes for keeping jewels, gold and silver were goldsmiths – jewellers. People used to ask them to look after their gold and silver for them. The goldsmith would give a receipt for that, which said that so-and-so had deposited five pounds worth of silver with him, for example.

Five pounds worth of silver used to be a large amount of money, for the pound was originally a pound weight of silver coins. Even at the beginning of the twentieth century it was a lot. For hundreds and thousands of years before that the values of gold and silver had not changed much except for fluctuations in unusual times. Then they would return to their normal value when the unusual situation had passed.

In the 20th and 21st centuries, the value of money has been changing at an incredible speed, constantly plummeting. We in the West do not see the effects of that quite as much as some do. Some countries see prices going up quickly all the time.

Many people used to keep their valuable gold, silver and jewellery with the goldsmith and so he had quite a lot in his safe. People did deals with each other and so sometimes, rather than pay each other money, they made an agreement that the money to be paid would stay at the goldsmiths. Ownership of it passed to the person whom the buyer wanted to pay for his purchase. The buyer paid the other person with the receipt that he had from the goldsmith. The other person could take the receipt and collect the gold if he wanted, or he could leave it with the goldsmith for safekeeping. The goldsmith's safe is one of the beginnings of the bank and his receipt is one of the beginnings of the banknote. It is no accident that one of the oldest banking families in Europe is called Goldsmith.

Merchants
Some of the great merchants would later turn into bankers. Trade has always been the most profitable form of economic activity and merchants the wealthiest section of society. The merchants were approached for loans which they granted and on which they charged interest. Very often they found it easier and more profitable to lend money than to trade and so some merchants gradually evolved into bankers. The Medici are good examples of this process.

There were other models, which Shakespeare records in the character of Antonio in his **The Merchant of Venice**. Antonio abhors usury and lends money to his friend Bassanio without interest. Later, out of concern for Bassanio's wish to marry, he undertakes responsibility for Shylock's loan to Bassanio, which ordinarily would have been usurious, and around which the play revolves. The loan is non-usurious but in the event of failure is to be redeemed with a 'pound of flesh' taken from Antonio's body.

The setting for the story, Venice, had been a prosperous merchant city trading with both the Eastern Roman Empire in Constantinople and the Muslims. It had always financed its trade by profit-sharing 'commenda' much like Muslims' qirad loans. That was until Vasco da Gama forged an alternative trade route around the Cape of Good Hope in 1497-98. This changed the patterns of world trade. As we saw, it undermined the 'Silk Road' that was the basis of Ottoman, and Venetian, trade and prosperity. It changed the fortunes of Venice, which, for the first time, invited Jews to move in because they were hitherto unparalleled as bankers.

Scriveners
The last group to become today's bankers were the scriveners — the writer clerks — who recorded contracts between merchants and between borrowers and lenders. They came to occupy a position of power, because they could bring borrowers and lenders together, and so some of them evolved into bankers.

The creation of credit from nothing
If we return to the goldsmith, we see that this transaction of his was also the beginning of something strange but true, however odd it might seem. The goldsmith found that people only occasionally wanted their gold and silver back. They could buy and sell using the receipts he had given them, which they did, and so they didn't need to carry the valuable metals around. It was sometimes unsafe to carry gold and silver; there were pickpockets, highway robbers and burglars.

That gave the goldsmith a unique opportunity. People used to come to him to borrow money, sometimes because of difficulties and sometimes because of business ventures. The goldsmith really ought not to have lent other people's gold but he didn't want to risk his own. Real businessmen take risks. Bankers make sure that they take none with their own money, if they can help it.

He said to the borrower, "I have given people receipts for their gold and silver. They use them to buy and sell and everyone is happy with this. I am not going to lend you any gold or silver but what I will do is write a receipt for you which says that you have gold and silver in my safe-keeping. This is just as good as money. You must repay me this amount and a little bit extra for the **use**."

The goldsmith charged for the 'use' of the money and so it was called 'usury'. The word itself didn't originally mean something bad, even though the transaction was prohibited by Jews and Christians and is still prohibited by Islam. The word 'usury' was actually a euphemism.

People have been changing the meanings of words. Usury originally referred to charging 'any' interest at all on a loan. The deal is so bad and causes so much misery that usury thus came to be a bad word. Today its meaning has been revised to indicate 'extortionate' interest on a loan.

The word usury has today become old-fashioned. It is thought of as something that happened in olden days, but pay-day cash companies charge interest at rates well over a 1000%. Even what were once 'extortionate' rates of interest are no longer consider usury.

Calvin was the man who changed the idea of usury from meaning 'any interest' to meaning 'extortionate interest'. He said that perhaps less than 4% might not be too harmful, in certain circumstances, if it didn't cause too much difficulty to the borrower. More than that was 'usurious', it was extortionate. Very quickly other rebels against the Catholic church took advantage of this, but people like Henry VIII of England redefined 'usurious' in legal terms as anything above 10%. Today if the bank charges 12% or 18% and credit card companies almost 30% it is no longer thought to be extortionate. Here the meanings of the words have been changed radically and are still changing all the time. The example of loans at 1000% interest or more means that there is no longer any meaning to the word 'usury' and the law does nothing at all to regulate this extortionate behaviour.

That is a grave matter but we are ignoring something much more serious. The goldsmith had not lent the borrower anything at all! He had merely written a pretend note. It was a confidence trick, but it worked, usually. By trial and error, goldsmiths found that they could lend sometimes as much as sixteen times the amount they actually held in their safes. If they had £100 in real gold and silver, they could lend £1,600.

This worked as long as nobody suspected. If anybody became suspicious and panic spread, then everybody would want their money back at the same time. That was impossible. They wanted £1,600 and the goldsmith had £100.

If panic didn't happen, then the borrower paid the money back with interest. At that, the goldsmith could cancel out the false money he had invented by tearing up some of the receipts and just take his interest.

But throughout history people have at certain moments panicked. They wanted their money back "now, before the whole thing collapses." Then not only was the goldsmith in trouble, but everybody was in trouble. People had been using money that wasn't really there. What happens is called a 'crash'. Many go without work and money for a long time hoping only that someone will give them a bowl of soup. This happened in the nineties in Asia and in Russia and in the famous world crash of 2008. Crashes will continue to happen in America and Europe, and all over the world as long as this system exists. The system of lending more money than is in the bank is called 'fractional reserve banking'. That is a scientific term for forgery.

This extraordinary situation usually happens when there is enough of everything to go around, and yet countless numbers of people live in poverty for long periods of time. When William Cobbet, a 18th-19th century social commentator, saw the beginnings of this situation, he wrote: "...it has produced what the world never saw before; starvation in the midst of abundance."

People used to exchange something of value for goods. It is only the goldsmith, merchant or scrivener turned-banker in our story who takes a little extra every time. Gradually, because of his charging interest, more and more of the money became the property of this proto-banker. In the case of the goldsmith who already had gold, more and more of the gold became his property.

Everyone else became accustomed to using paper, just as today when ordinary people don't use much gold at all. In 1933, in the early years of the Great Depression, President Franklin D. Roosevelt signed an executive order granting the US government the power to purchase all its citizens' private gold at an artificially low price. Today some of it is said to be stored in the vaults of the Federal Reserve Bank of the USA. Some of it is in Fort Knox, and other places like the Bank of International Settlements.

Many people say that they think we should all begin to use gold and silver again. The bankers who argue against them say, "People have used all sorts of things as money (That is true). People have used salt (That is true). Even the Chinese used paper a long time ago (That is true). There is nothing special about gold and silver (That is a lie)."

The proof that it is a lie is that they have gone to a lot of trouble to get hold of almost all the gold on the planet. That only paper is legal tender has been enforced by legislation. Bankers have stashed gold away safely for themselves. If it really is unimportant to them whether we use gold or paper then let them put their gold up for sale and allow people to choose whatever they want to use. Let them see whether people choose to keep their paper or buy gold and silver and use them again.

Where does debt come from?

We often think that only we have debts. We think that it is just me, or my family, or my business, or my country, or the third world. That is not the case. Everybody has debts. The richest people have the biggest debts. The wealthiest nation — the USA — has the most enormous national debt. It is much bigger than any other country's.[1]

Originally, receiving interest for a loan was not allowed by Jews and Christians. That was revealed to their prophets, just as it was revealed to our Prophet, may Allah bless him and all the prophets and grant them peace.

The Children of Israel

The Children of Israel had a verse in their book which has caused a lot of trouble in history. This is in a book from the Old Testament called Deuteronomy. It says there that one should not take usury from a brother but it is permitted to take it from a stranger. Some people say that the Hebrew word for stranger in the verse means 'enemy'. This verse is almost certainly one of those that has been altered. But it has been said that, if it was a true revelation from Allah, the Children of Israel were allowed to charge usury to their enemies as an act of war.

Allah tells us in the Qur'an that some rabbis altered their revelations. This is one of the reasons that Allah sent new revelations with new prophets, and finally sent Sayyiduna Muhammad, may Allah bless him

1   At the end of the 2014 financial year the total government debt in the United States, including federal, state, and local, was expected to be $21.0 trillion.

46

and grant him peace, as the Seal of the Prophets. The revelation that Allah gave him – the Qur'an – has never been altered.

The rabbis may have altered this verse of their revelation to allow themselves the right to charge interest to their enemies. In Islam you may not charge interest to your enemies. If there are genuine enemies they can be fought for the sake of Allah, but the shari'a cannot be altered. We think that some rabbis invented this part of the verse in Deuteronomy. Our proof that this verse was altered is that Allah blames them for taking usury. Allah blames the rabbis for not telling the Children of Israel not to take usury. This is what we think, but Allah knows best.

We know from the Prophet, peace be upon him, that usury is a terrible thing which Allah hates. Usury is one of the worst things one can do after **shirk** – ascribing a partner to Allah. It is one of the wrong actions, such as murder, that are grave.

Some of the Children of Israel worked with usury from ancient times, long before Islam. In Europe they were early money-lenders and bankers.

The Christians

The Christians knew that usury is forbidden by Allah. For example, the Catholic Church had a law called Canon Law, in which usury was forbidden. People who charged usury were not treated as Christians when they died and could not be buried in a Christian graveyard. However, someone who had agreed to pay usury was not punished.

Our Prophet, peace be upon him, said that all of the people involved in usury are cursed: the one who charges usury, the one who pays it, the one who writes the contract down and the one who acts as a witness to the contract. The Christians never understood this. They could not see that the man who agrees to pay usury is as bad as the man who charges it. Therefore some Christians made use of Jewish bankers and moneylenders. They borrowed money from them and paid them interest. Many people did that: kings, bishops, merchants, and ordinary people. The Christians were hypocritical and they hated the Jews because some of them were usurers. In addition to the heroic merchant Antonio, Shakespeare treated this theme of usury in his **Merchant of Venice** in which Shylock was hated as a Jewish usurer but made use of by Christians nevertheless.

A debt with usury grows continually bigger and bigger. It is often impossible to pay it back. More and more people fall into debt. If the king or the government is in debt, they tax people to pay the debt, or to pay the interest on the debt. That makes it more difficult for people to pay their own debts as well as the taxes. They become frightened and angry. Sometimes there are rebellions and revolutions. The French Revolution was caused by a terrible national debt that grew continually and could not be paid and which caused dreadful suffering in France. Most of the poor French people were hungry for years on end.

Often the Christians would turn on the Jews because of the usury of their moneylenders and would kill them or drive them out of town or out of the country. As well as doing that all their money would be taken from them. Before the First Crusade, the Crusaders went around Europe killing Jews and taking all their money. This has happened again and again in Christian history.

For example, in Limerick, Ireland, in 1904 a boycott was instigated by a local priest, together with the townspeople to drive the Jews out of town for a variety of reasons including the usury that their moneylenders practised. This episode and others like it have less to do with racial hatred and more to do with debts which Christians owed Jewish bankers. Nevertheless, undoubtedly Christians often mixed up many issues in the toxic and emotional way that today we call 'anti-semitism'.

Then some Christians discovered something important. They realised that the secret of usury is not complicated, although certainly Jewish bankers had been the cleverest at it. Some decided that they might as well do it themselves. Some of the earliest bankers in Europe were thus

Italians and Germans. They included the Medici and the Fuggers.

The Muslims

The Muslims are the only people with a clear revelation who today really remember that usury is forbidden, and have a shari'a which shows how to trade and do business without usury. Unfortunately, many Muslim rulers and businessmen have done the same as the Christians and the Jews and have accepted the existence of usury.

Allah, exalted is He, is clear about how serious usury is. We have the Sunna of the Prophet, peace be upon him, and the Sunna of the Khulafa who took the right way after him. The Prophet was a trader before Allah revealed the Qur'an to him. When he emigrated to Madina and established the mosque there, he also established a market for the Muslims to trade in. Rent was not to be charged for a place in the market nor were Muslims who traded in it to be taxed.

The people of Madina grew dates and other crops. Many of the emigrants from Makka were experienced traders who had gone on caravans to Syria and the Yemen.[2] When Allah revealed that usury is forbidden they all took great care to learn how to trade without using interest and other types of usury. It is such a serious matter that they went to great lengths to try and avoid usury.

Islam is not like Judaism and Christianity in many ways. One important difference is that the Jews and the Christians have lots of legends and stories and not enough history about their prophets. Although the Muslims also have some legends and stories, the early Muslims worked hard to record the history of Sayyiduna Muhammad, may Allah bless him and grant him peace, and his Companions in Madina.

In particular, Muslims recorded the Sunna and details about how the Companions traded in the market without usury. They also made

2   See **The Year of the Elephant,** by Abdassamad Clarke. Ta-Ha Publishers Ltd.

a record of the various ways in which usury can enter into transactions if one is not careful, in order for people to be on guard and prevent it from happening.

Our Prophet, may Allah bless him and grant him peace, did not earn his living by trading after Islam, but he understood trade and was watchful over the marketplace. The Companions knew that at any moment an ayat of Qur'an might be revealed about what they were doing, and so took as much care in buying and selling as in their prayers and worship.

One entire sura changed the way people thought about trade. Before Surat al-Mutaffifin was revealed, the people of Madina used to think that religion was for the mosque, but that trade in the market was a different matter. After its revelation it was understood that one has to be as careful in one's trade as in prayer.

We know a lot about the Sunna of trade from the way that the Companions bought and sold.

Islam is the last revelation to mankind until the end of time. Allah made sure that we would have everything in Islam we need for all times to come and in all parts of the earth. People who say, "That was those days, but now we live in the modern age and in Europe or America and things are different" have not understood the time we live in. Islam fits the way the world will be until the end of time.

Judaism is the remnant of an ancient revelation that was meant for the Children of Israel. Sayyiduna 'Isa, peace be upon him, was a prophet sent to the Children of Israel. That means that his teaching was for people who were following the shari'a of Musa, peace be upon him. The Apostle Paul never met 'Isa. He took Christianity to the Romans and the Greeks and he did not tell them about the shari'a of Musa. He only told them to 'believe' in 'Isa and not to worry about the law. The Christians thus had a belief without a law but even their belief system, their creed, had a fatal flaw in it. Then, because no society can live without laws, the Christians adopted the Roman legal system when under Constantine and later emperors the Romans adopted Christianity as state religion.

Islam was revealed for all people across the earth at all times in history. The Sunna of buying and selling is simple and it is also sophisticated. It is adaptable to all circumstances. Inherent in it is that one cannot make an Islamic bank or what people call 'Islamic Economics'.

The Islamic bank

When Western countries came to dominate the Muslim world the Muslims were shocked. Many did not understand how that had happened. People thought that the non-Muslims had something clever. The Muslims wanted to find a way to do the same things which had made the non-Muslims so strong, in order for the Muslims to become strong again and leaders in the world. As Ibn Khaldun demonstrated in his book: the vanquished will always imitate their vanquishers.

A lot of people then said that we must have things like Islamic parliaments, Islamic democracy, Islamic science, and Islamic economics and Islamic banks.

That was a mistake. Some Muslims think the reason that non-Muslims are stronger is because they have something better, whereas Muslims today are weaker for a variety of reasons including the fact that they have not understood that paper and digital money themselves are the trick and that they are usury.

To make an Islamic bank is only to become more caught up in this error. Islamic bankers and Islamic economists believe that fiat money is permitted but they worry about the interest payments which are forbidden. You have already seen that fiat money is much more serious than interest payments even though interest is serious enough. But we will return to the Islamic bank in greater detail later.

Taxes — the Second Inevitable

"Two things in life are inevitable: death and taxes."
Benjamin Franklin

It has become almost inconceivable for many people that one might live under a regime that does not tax one, yet "...an income tax was established (generally between 1910 and 1920 but in some countries, such as Japan and Germany, as early as the 1880s" (Thomas Piketty, Capital in the Twenty-First Century). In other words the most common form of taxation today was established around 100 years ago and is thus a recent historical phenomenon.

Distinctions of East and West, North and South are becoming increasingly irrelevant. As the world hurtles towards what a recent NASA sponsored report flagged as an irreversible collapse whose basis is: "the stretching of resources due to the strain placed on the ecological carrying capacity"; and "the economic stratification of society into Elites [rich] and Masses (or "Commoners") [poor]" addressing that 'economic stratification' is becoming increasingly urgent for all our sakes. As we shall see, contemporary taxation contributes substantially to that stratification.

The Spectrum of Taxation
The spectrum of taxation according to Islam is represented by two extremes: first, the numerous texts from the Qur'an and the Prophetic practice obligating the payment of zakat, and its collection and distribution by collectors appointed by those in authority; second, the prohibition of taxation on trade except for customs tariffs on traders from outside the Muslim polity.

Value Added Tax or Maks

Maks is a percentage, usually 10%, taken from traders in the market place. An-Nawawi said, "... maks is an act of disobedience and a mortal wrong action." In other words, maks is a VAT, except that European VAT is now more than double that on average. The only legitimate reason to collect something from market traders is for the upkeep of the market itself.

Zakat

A central raison d'être of governance is to bring about the communally obligatory aspects of the acts of worship, most importantly the prayer and the charitable tax, zakat. The person in authority must take wealth from the prosperous and wealthy and give it to eight deserving categories, most prominent among whom are the poor and the needy. Even though zakat in itself will not deal with all disparities of wealth and income or solve the seemingly intractable problems of poverty, it serves a very significant role in that it very publicly articulates the importance and centrality of these issues. The role of governance is to maintain that focus on the welfare of the general populace by maintaining the high profile of zakat in the society. Like all individual obligations, it is better that zakat is done as publicly as possible, so that, like justice, not only is it done but it is "seen to be done". We assume the reader's understanding that the 'person in authority' can be anyone from the leader of a small Muslim community to a king or sultan ruling a large polity.

Although zakat is collected by knowledgeable people with integrity who are appointed by those in authority and is not merely a voluntary charity, it is not state revenue. It may not be used for governmental expenses and projects in any way, no matter how worthy. The only possible exception is that those who collect and distribute zakat are eligible to receive some portion of it. The logic of this is obvious. If they received no recompense it could conceivably undermine the collection and distribution itself or expose them to pressures that could result in their corruption.

Zakat may not even be used for noble or important projects such as building mosques, madrasas and hospitals, or roads, sewerage systems and other infrastructure. Nor can it be used as salaries for the leader and his administration. It must be spent locally and not sent far afield, except when there are no valid recipients locally such as needy or poor people, travellers, indebted people, slaves, 'hearts to be reconciled' or people engaged in fighting in the way of Allah. In that case, the zakat may be sent to the nearest needy locality. It may not be sent to recipients on the other side of the earth, even famine victims. That is the obligatory zakat. It is of course highly praiseworthy to send voluntary contributions to people in need and distress. But the principle of attending to those nearest and then the next nearest means that zakat is free from the paradoxical effects of charity, such as its undermining the economies of the very people that it is trying to help.

Jizya

Clearly Muslim governance had a great many other revenue streams that were not so restricted. The first of these other sources of income is the jizya, that poll tax taken from adult non-Muslim males who, whether through force of arms or peaceful treaty, have made an agreement to live under Muslim governance according to the contract known as the dhimma. This tax has become a historical bone of contention because it is felt to be 'discriminatory' and 'humiliating', and yet it was ordinarily something in the region of four gold dinars paid annually, i.e. approximately 600 euros, and those who paid it were exempt from paying zakat. It was dropped or reduced in cases of penury and indeed needy non-Muslims were given from the public treasure (bayt al-mal) in such cases. There are many today who would queue up to be able to pay such a low annual tax.

Custom Duties – 'Ushr – A Tenth

An additional legitimate revenue for the polity are those taxes, usually 10%, collected from the trade of people residing outside the Islamic polity who enter to trade.

Kharaj

A very substantial tax was the kharaj tax paid on land that had come under Muslim governance whether by treaty or through military victory. It could be paid in kind or in cash. It was roughly equivalent to the amount paid in zakat by Muslims, non-Muslims being exempt from paying zakat. During the caliphate of 'Umar, the fighting men had wanted to divide up the conquered lands into their personal landed estates, but 'Umar refused. Some of the most substantial lands in terms of income were the Iraqi lands known as as-Sawad, rich fertile land that sustained massive date groves.

"...when Abu Hurayra brought 500,000 dirhams of jizya and kharaj from Bahrain, a previously unheard of sum, 'Umar accepted the counsel of one of the Companions and instituted diwan-registers of the Muslims and set up stipends for them." This was the beginning of the opening of the floodgates of income whose midpoint was the transformation of as-Sawad of Iraq into a gigantic waqf for the Muslims. 'The kharaj of as-Sawad and al-Jabal at the time of 'Umar, may Allah be merciful to him, amounted to 120 million waf[1] and the waf is one dirham[2] and two and a half daniqs'.[3] (Ibn Sa'd, at-Tabaqat al-Kubra)

"The furthest point at this stage was reached in the history of the khilafa of 'Uthman when, as as-Suyuti wrote in Tarikh al-Khulafa: 'In the year 30 AH, Jur was opened and many provinces of the land of Khurasan; Naysabur

1   The weight of ten dirhams is equal to the weight of seven dinars. A waf (full) dirham has the same weight — a mithqal — as a dinar.

2   The dirham weighs 2.975g and its value is $7.00 USD, 5.50 EUR or £4.34 GBP (27/9/2013).

3   The daniq is a sixth of a dirham. So the waf is 1.416 dirhams. The kharaj was thus 169,960,000 dirhams worth £737,626,400 or just under a £1 billion. Bear in mind that today silver is grossly undervalued for a variety of reasons so that this sum only represents a fraction of the real value of the kharaj.

was opened by treaty, and it has been said, by force. Tus and Sarkhas were both opened by treaty, and similarly Marw and Bayhaq. When these extensive provinces were taken, 'Uthman's revenues became abundant, and wealth came to him from every direction.'" (The Muslim Faculty of Advanced Studies, Autumn 2013 module: Muslim History, Early Madina, the lecture on Jihad)

'Umar had dealt with this previously unheard of wealth by establishing what was in essence a gigantic waqf-endowment for the well-being of the community from which people were given stipends according to their ranks and precedence in Islam, starting with the wives of the Prophet, peace be upon him, then the men who had fought at the Battle of Badr and so on.

The revenues from jizya and kharaj have no restrictions placed on their usage such as those that pertain to zakat. They can legitimately be used for more general public welfare and administration. As we saw, the caliph 'Umar largely devoted them to the general welfare of all the community to lift them from penury and free them from some measure of the pressure of earning a living.

Royal Authority and Dynasty

It is commonly thought that the deterioration of Muslim civilisation began with the establishment of kingship and the siphoning off of funds to maintain lavish royal lifestyles, but Ibn Khaldun argues the necessity of kingship and some degree of regal splendour. Since a fundamental purpose of Islam is the application of the law without which justice is impossible, then royal authority as the guardian of law needs to be respected for the sake of the law itself. Ibn Khaldun cites an instance in the very first community that goes straight to the point.

When Mu'awiya, in the splendour of kingship and its manner of dress and equipment, met 'Umar ibn al-Khattab on his arrival in Syria, 'Umar repudiated that and said,

"Royal Persian behaviour (Kisrawiyya), Mu'awiya?" So he said, "Amir al-Mu'minin, I am on the frontier facing the enemy directly and we need to compete with them with the adornments of war and jihad." So he was silent and did not find fault with him since he had advanced an argument based on the purposes of the truth and the din. If his purpose had been to repudiate kingship in principle, the argument about this Persian royal behaviour and his assumption of it would not have satisfied him but on the contrary he would have urged him to leave it entirely. 'Umar only meant by royal Persian behaviour that which the Persians had in their kingdom such as perpetration of falsehood, injustice, tyranny and the behaviour of its young men (shibl) and forgetfulness of Allah. But Mu'awiya answered him that the purpose in that was not royal Persian behaviour and their falsehood but his purpose in it was only the Face of Allah, and so he ['Umar] was silent. (My own translation)

This is an argument that is central to Ibn Khaldun's thesis. The transition from the visionary society of 'Umar, in which the entire resources of the community were dedicated to general welfare, to one in which there was some measure of ostentation on the part of the élite was necessary.

Nevertheless, given the human capacity for envy and resentment, it has always been the case that, firstly, few later inhabitants of the palace ever understood the necessary role of royal authority in maintaining law and society and came to regard its revenues as their personal prerogative, and secondly and subsequently, sizeable segments of the population came to aspire to the life that they perceived kings and sultans to be living. In Europe this almost subterranean envy was to contribute substantially to the next phase.

The State

It is necessary to understand a further transition in order to confront our current situation: the rise of the 'state'. This is a peculiarly European phenomenon that has been universalised even to the extent that some people who have not understood its provenance claim the need for an 'Islamic state'.

In the breakup of the European order of the Hapsburg Empire and the Roman Catholic Church during the struggles brought about by the Reformation, a resolution of the terrible Thirty Years War was achieved in 1648 by a series of treaties known as the Peace of Westphalia that defined states in terms of peoples' sovereigns. This new mapping of political order took its next most significant step during the French Revolution 1789-1799. The state was no longer to be based on the sovereign but on the 'nation' or 'the people', in this case the French nation. But this was an entirely spurious entity with no reality. 'France' was inhabited by a wide variety of peoples with a number of cultures and speaking all sorts of different languages. As Shaykh Dr. Abdalqadir as-Sufi demonstrated in his masterpiece **The Time of the Bedouin**, the inevitable consequence of positing the 'nation' was the genocide of those who did not fit the national profile. Far from exterminating the aristocracy, the Revolution turned upon many inconvenient groups in France and obliterated them in a most terrible fashion.

That pattern has been repeated wherever the fever for the nation-state alighted. It was one of the significant factors in the breakup of the Osmanlı polity. Every Balkan grouping, Serbs, Croats, Bosnians, Macedonians, Greeks and Albanians, wanted their nation-state with the result being the extermination or expulsion of those populations that did not fit within the paradigm. This is also true of Turkey which went from being a land with a rich mix of Muslims, Christians and Jews and a polity that easily absorbed Kurd and Albanian, to an almost exclusively Turkish entity with a lingering 'Kurdish problem'.

In Europe this development was also accompanied by the appearance of the new middle classes who aspired to some portion of the life of luxury they imagined royalty and aristocracy to be enjoying. Thus everyone wanted a bit of the state revenues and, where that was not possible, they proved to be customers for the banks that evermore advanced into the forefront of civic life.

With the transformation that the agricultural revolution brought about globally and the surge of rural populations into the new cities and megalopolises, the state took on an entirely new character, becoming the employer and sustainer of massive populations, so that today in the EU, perhaps a half or more the populace work for the state, even if in the ignominious role of being unemployed. Thus, there are few who are going to argue about the need for taxation since it contributes directly to their livelihoods.

The Bank

Parallel to the rise of the states grew the banks and national banks that were to become inseparable from them and which were to finance state expenditure and, as a consequence, take a substantial part of tax revenue in repayment and to 'service the debt', i.e. pay interest on it. In the UK, "In 2012, the annual cost of servicing the public debt amounted to around £43bn, or roughly 3% of GDP.... Each household in Britain pays an average of around £2,000 per year in taxes to finance the interest."[4]

In addition, economist Margrit Kennedy calculated that almost 45% of the prices people pay for those things they need to live are composed of interest.

We speak of course in the context whose quotidian reality, East and West, among Muslims and non-Muslims, is that the state exempts the super-wealthy from taxation but instead taxes those whom the shari'a counts among the needy. Many income earners are counted by shari'a as needy, for a needy person is anyone who cannot make ends meet

4   https://en.wikipedia.org/wiki/United_Kingdom_national_debt#Cost_of_servicing_the_debt

even if they own their house and have a business or livelihood or, in a more precise definition, someone who does not have year's provisions for himself and his dependents. A great many of the world's working people today would be counted as needy and not required to pay zakat but would, on the contrary, be eligible to receive it.

This sheds light on the otherwise inexplicable hostility shown Islam and Muslims today by the media and the political class; Islam is perceived as being inimical to the vested interests of power and wealth. Yet, this is absurd because Islam is not a socialist resentment of power and wealth but, indeed, honours them both. It is one of the core values of Islam, 'the purposes of the shari'a — maqasid ash-shari'a', that the preservation of wealth is a good thing and Muslims have always embraced the world, commerce and trade with alacrity. Arguably this has been the undoing of many Muslims in the present age because of lack of understanding of the banking and finance that are based on fiat money and on usury.

Income Tax — Dariba
Thus we come to not a tax instituted by Islam but a tax which Islam can throw some light on and which is the outcome of the previous developments. The modern term for income tax — dariba — is used in a context that makes it very revealing. In classical times it was very common for slaves to have certain skills that were useful in the world and the marketplace. They were ordinarily allowed to go out and practise their skills and earn money, and usually they worked towards purchasing their freedom. A part of the arrangement was that the master could negotiate an impost that his slave had to pay him, a dariba.

Income tax in itself is of very recent origin. In the UK, it was first imposed in 1799 during the Napoleonic Wars as an emergency measure and, once the wars had passed, it was rescinded in 1816. It was re-introduced by Robert Peel in 1842. It had a chequered history of being re-instituted for emergencies, whether military or budgetary, and rescinded but was finally imposed during the First World War and never again abolished. A relic of its provisional nature is the annual ritual of the British Budget, whose raison d'être is to prove that the exigency that necessitated this extra burden on the citizens is still in effect. Of course, there are few serious people who know this arcane fact yet alone call for the abolition of income tax.

Thus we arrive at a point in history in which taxation has reached unprecedented levels and yet so many are dependent on it as recipients that there is no one to object. Exactly who is taxing who and for whom? Of course, the presence of banking within the equation has not yet fully received the attention it deserves. Nevertheless, the peril of such massive taxation is that it proves an impediment to the very cultural and economic life it lives off and thus ordinarily brings down the society itself.

Ibn Khaldun on Excessive Taxation

"... when the dynasty follows the ways (sunan) of the religion, it imposes only such taxes as are stipulated by the religious law, such as charity taxes (sadaqat), the land tax (kharaj), and the poll tax (jizya). They mean small assessments, because, as everyone knows, the charity tax on property is low. ... When tax assessments and imposts upon the subjects are low, the latter have the energy and desire to do things. Cultural enterprises grow and increase, because the low taxes bring satisfaction."[5]

He then details how illegal taxes creep in so gradually that people hardly notice and they become an accepted part of the economic and social fabric but in the end bring down the whole edifice of the culture because the desire to do or make anything is inhibited by the burden of taxation:

"Eventually, the taxes will weigh heavily upon the subjects and overburden them. Heavy taxes become an obligation

5   Ibn Khaldun, al-Muqaddima, Trans: Rosenthal, vol.2, p.89

and tradition, because the increases took place gradually, and no one knows specifically who increased them or levied them. ...Finally, civilization is destroyed, because the incentive for cultural activity is gone. It is the dynasty that suffers from the situation, because it (is the dynasty that) profits from cultural activity."[6]

But none of this is inevitable and Ibn Khaldun cites examples such as Salah ad-Din al-Ayubi and Yusuf ibn Tashfin who abolished onerous taxation and restored the light taxation of Islam. It is the contention of this small article that redressing the current imbalances and excesses in taxation are in the interest of both rich and poor and the future of our globalised society.

6   Ibid, pps.90-91

The State

Modern man thinks that he has to arrange existence. He has set up the state and supra-national bodies to plan everything. Economists and politicians think that they have to organise everything and that it is up to them to run the planet. That is really what Allah does. The Muslims understand that. Thus khalifate is not a 'world state'. We do not think that we would make better managers than others.

A Muslim stands in front of Allah and knows that he has a reckoning for what he does. Financiers, bankers, economists and others are trying to make a world state, unaware of that reckoning or even denying it. The Muslims try to serve Allah, avoid the Fire and enter the Garden. Now that could sound like a slogan, but it has real meanings.

First, the Muslim takes care that everything he does is halal and pleasing to Allah. He counsels and advises others to do what is right and good and to leave off what is wrong and bad. That was what the Prophet did, may Allah bless him and grant him peace. Countless noble men and women throughout history lived their lives as close to his life as they could and huge numbers still do. When people change in this way the whole society becomes safe and wholesome.

As a body, Muslims entrust some matters to others among them, leaders and judges for example. And those people deal with issues that pertain to the whole society, such as being vigilant about the market and its transactions.

Islam — governance without state

Many modern Muslims talk about an Islamic state. This was not what the Prophet brought, peace be upon him, but he did bring a way for the Muslims to govern themselves. Governance is not the same as a state. Muslims also governed Jews and Christians and other People of the Book who agreed to live under their rule. And under Muslim governance many Jews and Christians came to occupy high posts within the administration. The job of governance is not to manage the entire society but to put some specific things in place that will help in creating a just and merciful polity.

One of the first necessities of governance is an army. The Western tradition was originally based on armies of people conscripted to fight. This was a legacy from feudalism and the idea that people were somehow the property of their rulers. The state inherited the role of treating its people as its property and thus we had conscription until comparatively recently.

The modern state began to take on the idea of its citizens as being free politically but as being determined by economics. Thus, it has standing armies composed of professional soldiers whose only job is to fight and who receive a regular salary. What changes everything is the modern belief that people act out of self-interest and, in extremis, out of desire for money and that this is an acceptable situation. The belief in selfless public service has been undermined. The belief in divine service has vanished.

The belief that people are essentially selfish has been self-fulfilling. We have an utterly selfish society. Thus if modern people receive a salary for fighting, they must see to it that there is always fighting to be done in order to be sure of receiving their salaries. Standing armies often contribute to the creation of wars, although bankers are even better at that.

Jihad was a different way of warfare from the standing army. When the ordinary Muslim in the original situation was obligated to fight jihad he did not become a professional soldier and he did not get a wage for it. He might have died in the fighting, for which he hoped to enter the Garden without reckoning. He might have won the battle, and received his share of the spoils. After that he would go back to his business if there was no more fighting to be done. That is different from receiving a salary for fighting.

Muslims did introduce standing armies at quite an early point in history. Then they potentially became subject to the same dynamics. Yet they still had an ethos of divine service. The dynamic in which a profession becomes self-serving and self-perpetuating can also apply to jihad. The fighter may fight for the wrong reasons: glory and plunder. There is no real escaping the need for the human being to examine his heart.

The police

Another example. States have policemen. The policeman used to be a public servant making sure that doors were locked late at night, and that suspicious people didn't wander around causing trouble. This pertained until recently but has been radically transformed by the transformation of the state by the thesis that man is essentially selfish and motivated by the desire for gain.

The modern policeman is paid to find crime. His business is crime and if there were no crime and no criminals he would be out of a job. Yet policemen do not see today's biggest crime, which is the theft by banks and stock exchanges of people's wealth. This was originally a legal crime and not just a moral one. The law of the land has been redefined so that usury is now THE essential pillar of society. What was an abhorrent vice is now virtue itself.

All Muslims are responsible for each other's safety and well being. They are themselves law-abiding and they look to see that the law is obeyed in their society. The policeman or **shurti** is a public servant who carries out his tasks on behalf of others, not in order to control them. The soldier is someone who defends the frontiers of the polity.

Both are noble tasks that ought to be done for the sake of Allah and rewarded by the polity.

Bureaucracy

Institutions such as armies, police and tax-collectors need bureaucracies to run them. Bureaucracies, armies and police forces need salaries. The modern state can only pay these if it has taxation. Very often taxation is not enough to pay for all these things and so the government borrows. As we see elsewhere in this book, earlier states made national debts and then only paid the interest on the debt so that they didn't have to demand such high taxation, but quickly the interest grew and the taxation became much higher than they had wanted. Thus, our situation today.

The state and the bank

In Europe the first clients of bankers had been kings and, surprisingly, popes. Then banking spread downwards throughout society. Thus with the advent of mass society and the modern state, both the state and the masses became customers. This has transformed both the state and its people. It has transformed the very purpose of people's lives. Rather than eating in order to live, people are living, working and producing in order to consume. That is not because they are individually bad people but because the circumstances have been so altered it is almost impossible not to.

Islam is the deen of **fitr** – it is the natural way. With that natural way, people like the Ottomans ruled one of the greatest civilisations in the world. Their khalifate ruled Muslims, Jews and Christians.

Some of their later khalifas made a serious mistake and borrowed a great deal of money at interest. That is one of the reasons Ottoman civilisation began to collapse. One of the last great khalifas, Sultan Abdalhamid II, may Allah show him mercy, tried courageously to get rid of that debt and restore the Caliphate, but the enemies of Allah removed him. We must learn from the mistake of those khalifas who borrowed huge sums of money.

Socialism and Capitalism

Modern people think that our contemporary world is capitalist and that socialism is something different from it ,but both capitalism and socialism are varieties of the same view of existence and of economics. In 'capitalism' today, power has come to belong to wealthy private bankers and financiers who have great amounts of 'capital'. Under 'socialism', however, the state is supposed to own the capital. Remember that having a strong central bank is a central plank of socialism that is even listed in the Communist Manifesto. Both systems are built on the power of capital. Today's capitalists operate through layers of corporations and holding companies and arguably the state itself is just another corporate banking entity.

Socialism

Soviets, from the first days of their revolution, borrowed money from capitalist banks. The US supplied them with technology, most particularly weapons, and arranged loans for the purchase. This process was documented extensively by Professor Antony Sutton in the three volumes of 'Western Technology and Soviet Economic Development' that detailed the process from 1917-65. This is perhaps one of the core concepts that one needs to understand: banking comes into the process of the acquisition of technology almost surreptitiously. It is assumed that since almost no one questions the need for technology, then there must be a need for the modes of finance that have historically been used for acquiring it. But, the modes of credit are numerous and not all of them are usurious.

Even though they were supposed to be deadly enemies, the capitalists sold the Soviets technology and lent them money to buy it, right up until the end of the Soviet Union. It was those loans' inexorable growth that destroyed the Soviet Union.

Western bankers really liked the Soviets because they always paid the interest they owed on their debts. They paid until the day they became bankrupt. The socialists oppressed the Russian people and all the many Muslim peoples from the Soviet Republics and took heavy taxes from them to pay the banks.

The arms race

You might be surprised at that and say, "But both sides were almost at war and both sides were building incredible numbers of nuclear weapons and missiles to fight each other!" Exactly! The socialists borrowed most of the money to do that from Western banks. Remember: trade unites what politics divides. This is also true of usurious finance but in a much more sinister manner.

Ronald Reagan, an American president 1981-89, began what is known as the Strategic Defence Initiative or, more popularly, Star Wars. It was an elaborate final card in the poker game called the Arms Race.

Ever since the end of the Second World War, East and West had competed in building nuclear weapons. Even in the fifties and the sixties, both sides had enough weaponry to destroy each other's nuclear missile sites, naval bases, army camps, cities, industries and every living thing, and then do it five more times! That was only the beginning. Suitably, this insane situation was called M.A.D., an appropriate acronym for Mutually Assured Destruction. Because the destruction would be mutual neither side pressed the button.

Then the Americans thought of the idea of setting up a satellite system outside the atmosphere which would use lasers and other devices to shoot down foreign missiles: Star Wars. This wasn't going to cost nothing.

Because we now understand the deal that William of Orange did with the banks, we understand that the banks pay for it in the short term, and the American people will pay for the rest of their history, many times over.

If the Americans could shoot down all the Soviet missiles from outer space, they could afford to launch a few at the communists themselves without fear of retaliation. The Soviets obviously needed a similar defence system and therefore had to agree something with their bankers. A fortune was spent on both sides, but the whole thing was impractical. At best they would be able to shoot down 30% of the missiles. If they are nuclear missiles, one needs to eliminate them entirely. Although the immense amounts of weaponry still hang over the human race like the Sword of Damocles, the whole US-Soviet Union Arms Race has been forgotten by everybody except the bankers who are still collecting interest payments from both camps on the loans which both parties borrowed to pay for this madness.

In the meantime the Soviet Union went bankrupt. Why do you think that is? The US now has a national debt measured in trillions. The trillion is a thousand billions and the billion is a thousand millions. The US is technically bankrupt already, but bankruptcy is being postponed by the ingenious device of borrowing more money for more wars and making the debt even bigger.

Corporatism
The forms — the one in which private enterprise owned the capital and the other in which the state owned the capital — came to merge in both East and West. Private enterprise threw up corporate form, of which corporations, banks and the state itself are the prime examples. Now corporations, banks and the state are in collusion all over the world. Corporate capital has come to exceed state capital many times over. One American corporation, the supermarket chain Walmart, has an economy roughly the same size as those of Saudi Arabia and the Gulf states combined. It is an open secret that banks and corporations

are in charge and so the state obliges corporations with useful pieces of legislation. It also helps out with police and even military enforcement when needed.

"Of the 100 largest economies in the world, more than half are global corporations. The Top 200 corporations' combined sales represent over one quarter of the world's GDP."[1]

All the false oppositions that one could imagine between banks, corporations and the state disappear instantly when one realises that all of them are corporate in form. Arguably the state is already a part of the banking world through its central bank. The major manufacturing corporations are on their way to becoming banks. For a substantial period Ford made no money on the sale of cars, but were in profit because of the finance terms they could offer customers.

If we look carefully at what we have today, it is more accurately called 'corporatism', which is what happens when capitalists and the state collude to produce monopolies. This sinister term was coined by Mussolini who thought it was a good thing and considered it another name for the movement of 'fascism' which he founded. Others call this modern form 'crony capitalism' or 'crapitalism'.

Nevertheless, in spite of apparent conflicts and differences between different state actors such as the US and the Russians, they both share identical views of the world and of money and its role. Tellingly, the banks and corporations continue to do business on both sides even in the midst of apparent political conflict. Politics serves merely as a soap opera to divert our gazes from the real issue and economics is the theology of a new religion. This religion irreversibly divides left and right, conservative and socialist, republican and democrat, with a

1   David Morris, Director of The Public Good Initiative at the Institute for Local Self-Reliance, "Should Large Nations Split into Small Nations?"

mutual antipathy that is more extreme then anything shown to Muslims. It even tempts the unwary to articulate Islam in left/right terms and to step into one of the two set of shoes, at which point they also inherit the hostilities of that party. Thus, in another not entirely unrelated zone, many Muslims have unthinkingly taken over Christian Creationism and its hostility to Darwin and so the position of Islam itself on life and living forms remains entirely un-articulated.

Economics

Economics is the pseudo-science that validates the usury on which the game is based. Superficially it appears to be scientific but suffers the same defect that science in general suffers, but to a much more pronounced degree: it is based on a series of implicit assumptions that are completely wrong and are, in its case, completely inhuman.

Selfishness

The most fundamental assumption of economics is that people are basically selfish to an extreme degree. Economists think that society can be understood as comprising brutishly selfish people competing for scarce resources. Indeed, this view sees all altruism as being selfishly motivated. Far from being established truth, this is simply materialist doctrine. It is an untested hypothesis not an established fact or even a theory.

Economists posited and assumed selfishness, then the science of economics and the practice of usury turned the world into precisely the selfish and brutish world they envisaged. There is the terrible self-fulfilling nature of assumptions.

Scarcity

The second most fundamental assumption of economics is the scarcity of resources. In order to sustain this myth, votaries of economics, such as the mandarins of the EU, destroyed a great deal of food and contrived to keep other things off the market in order to maintain the scarcity without which the system they had devised would collapse. Similarly, the great De Beers diamond monopoly is an active conspiracy to buy up the world's diamonds and remove them from the market entirely. Yes, I did use that word: 'conspiracy'. De Beers do that to make sure that the price of a diamond, whose actual worth is £5, remains £500.

Supply and demand

Based on the above crude assumptions, the Law of Supply and Demand has passed into popular culture as if it were an unquestionable axiom, whereas it is simply a spurious hypothesis. It states that where there is a great deal of demand for a product of which there is little supply the price will rise. This is promoted as if an impersonal scientific law like the law of gravity. On the contrary, it is actually the statistical outcome of many individuals' behaviour. Each person's behaviour is based on their taking advantage of other people's need for something which is in short supply and raising the price. These people have choices and could choose to keep the price high even when the product is in abundant supply or, conversely, bring the price down when the product is in short supply.

The predictions of the law of supply and demand assumes that people are largely ungenerous and greedy or anxious and fearful. It takes no account of magnanimity (**ihsan**) which, certainly for Muslims and for most traditional or even healthy peoples, is a sizeable factor.

More seriously, it takes no account of the proper governance of markets in which a Muslim judge is required to consult with traders on the values of things, and then request traders who charge too little, in order to undercut other traders, or too much, in order to take advantage of shortages, to adjust their prices or leave the market.

It is genuinely difficult for modern people, including Muslims, to conceive of societies of people that are not motivated by greed and selfishness, and yet historically there have been entire societies like that.

Suffice it to say that the foundations of science have themselves been under intense scrutiny from scientists and philosophers for a considerable time. Science is not quite the all-wise arbiter of truth and falsehood that it is often thought to be. And economics is widely regarded as one of the least rigorous of the sciences.

Employment and contracts

U nemployment is the thing modern man fears, but employment is the lowest form of economic activity. Why is that?

We will look at how people traditionally lived. Society has always had two different types: free people and slaves. Free people earn their livelihoods in a number of ways. Indeed, slaves were often permitted to go into the market and practise their trades and crafts, earn money and make contracts to free themselves.

Warfare

One possible income is from warfare. This has been true throughout history. It is true for the ordinary infantryman to generals and career officers, and finally to the geopolitical forces for whom they fight and who reap the benefits.

Fighting in the way of Allah — jihad — is not a job and has no salary. One can be killed or one can win. If the fighter wins, he has a share in the spoils. But it is vitally important that he not fight for any worldly motive but to raise up the Word of Allah.

No prophet was ever allowed to take the spoils of battle before Sayyiduna Muhammad, may Allah bless him and grant him peace. The ancient Scandinavians used to throw the spoils of battle into bogs. Scandinavian bogs have yielded enormous amounts of treasure. We don't know that they were following a prophetic way. We do know that Allah says He sent prophets among all peoples. Some of the prophets we know, but most we don't know. In Islam the fighters were allowed to take a fixed share of the spoils for the first time in history, but only according to the strict rules of jihad.

Governance

A way of earning a living is if one is appointed by the person in charge to do some job of governance. Usually, there is some payment from the **bayt al-mal** for the person doing the work. It was unusual because Muslims traditionally had light governance with not a great need for bureaucracy as was also the case even here in the West before the last century.

Then there are other more ordinary ways of earning a living.

Crafts and manufacture

A noble class of professions is the crafts. To work with one's hands making things to sell is a noble livelihood. Muslim craftsmen and manufacturers were usually free, self-employed people. They often worked together with other craftsmen of the same trade in partnerships that were bound together in larger guild-like organisations, and as such they were not 'employed'. These guild-like organisations looked after a great deal of the social welfare of members and of their widows, heirs and other poor people. Guilds could also help in raising capital sums that members needed for new equipment or other necessities without charging interest for it.

Agriculture

Agriculture another important occupation. It is also interesting to us for another reason. In agriculture there is possible a non-usurious profit-sharing transaction, often called 'sharecropping'.

This word 'sharecropping' has a bad taste for modern people. It is almost identical to 'usury' in the minds of people who know a little recent history. That is because of the history of the abolition of slavery in America.

Christians and Jews did not have a good form of slavery. It could often be cruel. When it was abolished in America, however, it led to more degradation and even starvation.

Slaves had lived all their lives on the plantations and farms of their masters and had no experience of the world, unlike the slaves of Muslims who often worked and traded in the world. When American slaves became 'free', they had no capital with which to begin businesses nor land to farm.

Some landowners saw an opportunity, divided their land into smaller pieces and arranged to rent the land to the ex-slaves. This arrangement was called 'sharecropping', but it was different from the transaction the Muslims use.

Instead of paying a proportion of the harvest, the ex-slaves were asked to pay a fixed number of bags of the crop at the time of harvest. That meant that whether the harvest was good or bad the same amount had to be paid. The year when the harvest was bad, the ex-slaves were in real trouble.

The story gets worse. The ex-slaves had no tools to work with, no seed to plant, nowhere to live and nothing to live on. The same people 'lent' them all of these things, and each time the ex-slaves had to promise to pay a number of bags of the harvest, often leaving little or nothing for them and their families. Because of this many ex-slaves lived in desperate poverty. That is why sharecropping has such a bad name for western people.

Most of the ex-slaves travelled north to Detroit and other big cities and found work in the great factories that were springing up.

Because sharecropping was so evil, I often do not use the same term, but prefer to call it cropsharing.

Cropsharing in the shari'a means something different. It means that a person who owns land and fruit trees, for example, can make an agreement that another person who doesn't own land should work his trees. The second pays for that with a proportion of the harvest. If there is a good harvest, both do well. If there is a bad harvest, neither does so well.

This transaction is fair and generous to both parties. It is a part of the mercy of the shari'a.

Professions such as medicine

There are professions such as medicine and these pose interesting problems for us: what is the doctor selling? With the modern doctor it is not clear. For example, if the doctor is selling health, then patients only ought to pay when they receive health. This is a fundamental requirement of any ordinary transaction: we have to know what is being sold in return for what? Without clarity it is called **gharar** (uncertainty or risk) in Arabic and that is not allowed.

Traditionally, as with many such professions, sometimes the doctor would be paid from a **waqf** (charitable endowment) so that his work was a **sadaqa** from him and his payment was a **sadaqa** to him. Sometimes he could be paid from the **bayt al-mal** (public treasury). These are not the only alternatives. The only requirement is that it not be a deceptive or unclear transaction.

Employment

Another way Muslims can earn money is through 'employment'. However, this word means something different in the shari'a.

The most important thing in any transaction is that it should be clear. What is being exchanged should be stated clearly. As you have seen, most transactions are a kind of barter.

In employment or in any transactions you have to ask the question: what is being exchanged for what? You have already seen that payment today is paper or digital money. What is exchanged for it? Time! This is a type of transaction called **ijara,** except that paper and digital money are not recognised as adequate compensation in the shari'a.

But there must be more to modern employment than just selling time. After all, work does have to be done. Indeed, some modern contracts are flexible about the time worked. They focus more on the job being done, but still the overwhelming majority of jobs are paid by the hour, day, week, month and year.

The other part of the job is obedience. The employed person must obey during the hours in which they work. In that way the employed person is closer to the Islamic idea of a slave than a free person.

Shari'ah employment is a contract between two free people.

This is one reason why some say that it is forbidden for a Muslim to be employed by non-Muslims. If you work for a non-Muslim, you might have to practise usury on his behalf and other transactions that are not permitted. Allah, exalted is He, says, **"Do not obey the disbelievers nor the hypocrites."** Because they permit usury, Imam Malik also disapproved of Christians and Jews coming into the Muslims' markets. This is not because of some sectarian or racist dislike of other people but because such a relationship can lead to negation of the shari'a and of the justice it is set up to bring about.

But we have to admit the reality of the age in which we live. There are non-Muslims whose conduct is more honest and has more integrity than that of some Muslims. There are many such people who are striving energetically and with integrity to bring an end to usury and bring about a new society. Conversely some Muslims have completely imbibed the dog-eat-dog attitude of modern capitalism even though they might affirm Islam and even perform some of its obligations. There are no longer any easy and completely reliable formulas.

All Islamic contracts have to be clear, and transactions which are not clear are forbidden. The Islamic employment contract is clear. It is different from modern employment. It is for a job of work, for example, the job of clearing a garden, or cleaning a house. The important thing in **ju'l** is the work that has to be done, not the time the worker spends on it. In **ijara** the time can be the consideration for which a corresponding compensation is given.

The agreement is between two free people. There is the person who would like the work done, and there is the person who proposes that he or she would do the work. The agreement must please both of them. A lot of jobs happen once only. They are not repeated every week or every day and so there is no salary. The person who does the work should be paid before the sweat dries.

Slavery

A lot of things have been said about slavery. The Muslims did not invent slavery, but the shari'a doesn't get rid of it either. Allah, exalted is He, and His Messenger, may Allah bless him and grant him peace, have shown many ways to improve the lot of slaves.

Today, war creates refugees and prisoners of war. Everybody today has seen many terrible things about these unfortunate people. In war, the Muslims enslaved many of the people they conquered, but these slaves were not slaves of the empire, but rather worked in the homes of the Muslims becoming members of the family. Slaves were allowed to work, trade and marry.

Slaves also made contracts to buy their freedom, many masters made wills to free slaves when they died, masters who had done wrong actions freed slaves because of that and people freed slaves who would be able to manage in the world as a way of pleasing Allah. The freed slave was the **mawla** of his former master, and he continued as if a member of the family. The word 'mawla' means both 'master' and 'freed slave'.

Many slaves of talent quickly became important people in Muslim society, for example, a lot of the famous early Muslim scholars were slaves who had been freed. A large number of great khulafa were sons of slavewomen.

Once, the Ottomans captured a lot of English sailors and soldiers from an English ship and enslaved them. The English government sent a man called Captain Hamilton to arrange to ransom the prisoners. The sailors wouldn't come home because they had good lives, beautiful wives and had become more successful than was possible in England. Captain Hamilton had to return home alone.[1]

There is little doubt that slaves of Muslims often had a better life than 'free' people in the West. If we look at some of the contracts that we use today we see why. Modern employment is not the contract of a free person. It is sometimes much more akin to a sort of covert slavery.

Trade

One of the ways of earning a living that Muslims love most is trade. Later on we will look at how non-usurious profit-sharing is also allowed in trading as it is in agriculture.

The trader travels and buys goods in one place and takes them elsewhere to sell. He charges more than what it cost him, so that he covers his expenses and makes some profit. Merchants have always been some of the wealthiest people because they move food and other necessities around the world and people usually honoured them.

Muslim traders took Islam to places it had never before been. People say that after the time of the first great jihads, Islam was spread by traders and Sufis. Muslim traders used to work out their costs and then add on a reasonable profit for themselves. Such traders did not believe in 'supply and demand', and so did not ask for the price that could be got simply because of the product's scarcity in the marketplace. Their fairness and generosity made an impression on people and traders such

1   See **Islam in Britain 1558-1685,** Nabil Matar.

as the Yemenis took Islam to India, Malaysia, Indonesia, Bengal and the whole of East Africa.

Scholarship

Another way of earning a living is through scholarship. This presents an issue that has always been recognised as problematic. The scholar has the duty to be true to knowledge, to teach and propagate it, and to defend it when it is falsified, even when the ruler, the commercial class and the generality of people disagree.

Nevertheless, he must also pay his bills and pay his way in the world. If he is paid by the ruler, the traders or the population at large, he is less able to speak the truth. In the famous idiom: he who pays the piper calls the tune. Most people recognise this in the political realm and recognise corrupt scholars who are in the pay of governments and rulers. Nevertheless, we note that an honest person can still be paid in this way and retain his integrity even though it is difficult. What has always been a peril for Muslim scholars in addition to that are the dangers in the commercial realm.

Imam al-Ghazali noted that students love to study fiqh because it gives access to drawing up business contracts, dividing up wills and other things that yield money. Sometimes today, on the contrary, we bewail the lack of knowledge of fiqh of mu'amalat, the ordinary transactions aside from acts of worship, but there are many who know this area and many who are employed by banks to find ways to skirt the restrictions on usury.

The balance was achieved in societies such as Timbuktu whose scholars were merchants. They were financially independent of the amir and able to speak directly and fearlessly to him. It also meant that they were directly involved in keeping the market free of usury and other abuses. This also suggests an important way forward for the future: students of knowledge who go into business and hold to their knowledge, and businessmen who learn what is halal and haram about trade.

These are some of the ways in which Muslims traditionally earned their living. Because Muslims know that Allah is the Provider, our work is not to earn provision as such, but to earn halal provision in ways that are pleasing to Allah.

We will look in the next chapter in some more depth at how investment is permitted in the shari'a, and how it is abused in the modern world.

The Corporation

Many Muslims imagine that investments in stocks and shares are halal, because they take a part of the profits rather than fixed interest, as long as they do not involve alcohol or other things forbidden by the shari'a. This is not true. Let us look a little at this subject.

Shares and the stock exchange

Today, many small private companies finance themselves without shareholders by their own private capital or through loans from the banks or overdrafts. But, there appears to be a limit to how big such a company can grow, although limits are not necessarily a bad thing. Nevertheless, in a world of dinosaurs many people wrongly imagine that one has to be a dinosaur to survive, whereas it is, as we know, a guarantee of extinction.

Those companies that are ambitious become public companies by offering shares in the company to the public. The public then pays a certain sum of money for each share and that money belongs to the company and can be used for buying more machinery, employing more people, and buying more raw materials or parts for products. In return the company pays a dividend to the shareholders every year.

In Islamic law people cannot passively invest in a manufacturing company and then expect to pick up a profit each year. Investors can become active partners in the company, without hiding behind limited liability laws. The investors must themselves be partners. Even though it is profit-sharing rather than a fixed rate of interest, it is not allowed for a passive investor to simply pick up a regular profit. That begs the question: how did partnerships raise capital for new tooling and other needs? As we saw, the guilds often helped with the capital finance that members needed by offering non-usurious loans.

In modern law a company must pay a share of its profits to shareholders each year, if there are profits. When a company is set up like that, it must hold shareholders' meetings. The shareholders vote and elect people to sit on the 'board' of the company. Board members sometimes get a salary and sometimes shares in the company. They are in charge of the company.

These people are called 'Directors' and the board is called 'The Board of Directors'. Many of these people sit on lots of boards, for each of which they receive a salary or shares, sometimes receiving a salary for just a few hours of meetings each year. The directors choose people to manage the company, to do the actual work.

Control of a public company can easily be taken away from the people who first made it by voting within the board or at the Annual General Meeting at which shareholders elect board members. Often the founders will try to prevent that by owning a majority of the shares. Since people have votes according to the number of shares they have, those with the majority of shares will always win the vote.

The limited company
There is an invention of law called the Limited Company – 'Ltd' for short, and sometimes 'plc' which means 'Public Limited Company'. The key word here is 'limited'. This invention arose in 1855 in the UK. It mean that when people set up a limited company they are not entirely responsible for its debts when things go wrong.

Imagine three people who have a partnership calling themselves QXT Ltd. QXT Ltd is something different from the people who set it up, work in it and take their salaries and profits from it. It becomes, in the language of lawyers, a 'person', which is a strange concept with a lot of negative consequences. Such 'persons' are in fact thus licensed to operate in quite irresponsible ways and evade ordinary moral laws and some have interpreted the personality of such 'persons' as classical psychopaths. QXT Ltd will pay the partners their salaries and/or their shares of the profits. If QXT Ltd gets massively into debt and collapses, they have no responsibility, unless someone can show that they acted criminally or were negligent.

It is similar when QXT launches itself on the stock market and becomes the public limited company QXT plc. Many people become shareholders in QXT plc by buying its shares. They each receive a share of its profits if there are any. If there are no profits and it collapses, they lose their shares, but they are not responsible for QXT plc's debts.

This law is dishonest. But it is an accommodation that became necessary because of the paradoxical nature of money and wealth in our time. Companies can end up with inflated debts from money that has never existed and which is thus not repayable. Without limited liability status, the entire system would grind to a halt. But, when large companies go bankrupt, it affects many smaller companies which supplied it products and services. It often entails a string of subsequent bankruptcies.

For example, many small companies supply large supermarket chains with goods, usually on thirty days' credit, but sometimes sixty or more. That means that the supermarkets take the goods and pay for them thirty or sixty days later. If the supermarket goes out of business in that time, the smaller businesses will not get paid. Perhaps some time later when the lawyers and accountants have worked out all the details and sold what is possible of the company, the smaller company might then receive some small part of what it is owed. Often that is too late. In reality the lawyers and accountants are the first to be paid and the only ones sure to be paid in full. Many small businesses are thus driven bankrupt by the collapse of the bigger firm.

The corporation as person

One of the most startling aspects of this is that the company or corporation is legally considered to be a 'person'. As such, the directors and shareholders have limited responsibility for that person's debts. This act of anthropomorphism, invented to prevent creditors seizing company directors' assets to pay company debts, has astonishing consequences. We have all become accustomed to talking about corporate bodies as if they were persons with personalities – and remember that universities, governments both national and local, banks and corporations are all examples of corporate form. Political discourse talks about entities such as 'the US' and 'Russia' as if people with personalities. Banks such as Goldman Sachs or J. P. Morgan, and corporations such as Apple and Microsoft are discussed as if they were people. Indeed, Dr. Robert Hare, in the documentary 'The Corporation', shows that the personality traits of the corporation are those of the psychopath.

The company and corporation come about in part through the otherwise legitimate desire of people with money to invest their funds to good effect. In many ways, the culture of the Muslims is very much an entrepreneurial one.

Partnership – musharaka

In the shari'a, people can work as a partnership. If it is a physical partnership in a trade, the participants can do that if working in the same trade and do so in the same building, for example, tailors who ply their trade in a workshop together.

Similarly, if such people pool their capital together and set up in business, they can operate as a partnership in a number of ways. One way is to make joint decisions on how to operate their business. Another way is to pool their resources and trust each other to make independent decisions on behalf of all of them.

But, even if a group of people use a name such as QXT to work under, it is never something that really exists. **They** are QXT. If QXT has massive debts, the debts are theirs, and must be repaid if they can. Perhaps if they owe money to Muslims, they might forgive them their debts. It is good to forgive others debts which they cannot pay. A judge can rule that debtors are bankrupt with all its consequences.

Qirad or mudaraba — the profit-sharing transaction

There is one form of investment in Islam where someone can take a share of the profits without apparently doing work. If we examine it we will see that really the investor **does** work for his share of the profits. It functions in a different way from the modern stock exchange because it is for trade only and may not be used for manufacture.

A person may invest money with a trader for a purchase of some products, their transport to a new market and sale there for a mutually agreed share of the profits. When that deal is done the trader must return the investor's capital to him. Then the two parties divide up the profits between them, according to the pre-agreed percentages, after the agent's expenses. An investor may not leave his money with a trader year after year and expect to take a dividend. Although it looks like a passive way of earning money, nevertheless the investor has to be active in the market seeking out traders to invest in and evaluating them and the trading opportunities.

This transaction is called **qirad** by the people of the school of Madina (Malikis) and it is called **mudaraba** by people of the school of Iraq (Hanafis) and others. These are just the technical terms of the schools. In this book we use the terms used in Madina.

A story about qirad

There is a rather unusual case of qirad that happened in Madina.

Abdullah and Ubaydullah were two of the sons of Umar ibn al-Khattab who left with the army for Iraq. On the way home they passed by Abu Musa al-Ash'ari, the Amir of Basra in Iraq, who made them welcome. He asked if there was anything he could do to help them.

Then he said, "There is some property of Allah which I want to send to the Amir al-Muminin. I will lend it to you. You can buy wares from Iraq and sell them in Madina." Perhaps the sum of money was booty from jihad or from **jizya** collected from the People of the Book. It was safer to travel with wares than it was to travel with gold. This was his way of protecting the money. He said, "Then you give the principal to the Amir al-Muminin and keep whatever profit you make."

Abdullah and Ubaydullah said that they would like to do that. He gave them the money and wrote to Umar ibn al-Khattab, who was the Amir al-Muminin, to tell him to take the money from them.

When they came to sell the wares in Madina Abdullah and Ubaydullah made a profit, and then paid the principal sum to Umar. He said, "Did he lend everyone in the army the same as he lent you?" They said, "No." Umar said, "He made you the loan because you are the sons of the Amir al-Muminin. You must pay the principal sum and the profit."

Abdullah kept quiet. Ubaydullah said, "You do not have to do this, Amir al-Muminin. If the principal had decreased or been destroyed, we would have guaranteed it." You see that if they had carried the money as a trust and it had been lost or taken from them by force, they would not have been liable and would not have been responsible. Because they took it as a loan for business purposes, they became responsible for it. Umar just said, "Pay it!" Abdullah kept silent, and Ubaydullah repeated what he had said.

A man who was sitting there with Umar said, "Amir al-Muminin, it is better that you make it a qirad loan." Umar said, "I make it a qirad." He took the principal sum of the loan and half of the profit. Abdullah and Ubaydullah took half of the profit between them.

Umar didn't like his sons to be given special treatment because of who they were and because of who he was. Here Abdullah and Ubaydullah were lent a capital sum of money which allowed them to trade, do business and make a nice profit. The people of Madina already knew about the qirad loan. When the man sitting with him mentioned it, Umar recognised it right away and immediately decided that it was a qirad.

The usual form for a qirad is that the shares of the profits should be agreed before the money changes hands. The qirad loan itself must be paid in either gold or silver, another important reason for the re-introduction today of the dinar and dirham. The agent may pay for his travelling expenses from it. There are a number of other conditions, but it is not our purpose to explain it completely here.

Zayd and Everyman

Hitherto, we have examined grand geopolitical and corporate scenarios, but there is one character in this story we must yet look at, because he is the one who sustains the entire edifice and who, unbeknown to him, can change the entire situation: Everyman.

Everyman has suffered many vicissitudes throughout history in the east and the west. He has been coerced into wars not of his choosing, slaughtered by the enemy in defeat, sent to certain death by his own commanders on a whim. Chivalric mediaeval knights thought as little of exterminating him, his wife and children as they would of killing a fly; chivalry was reserved exclusively for other knights. Little has changed. He was press-ganged into the British Navy and sent far abroad perhaps never to return and sometimes to return many years later crippled or, alternatively, enriched somewhat.

With the appearance of the modern state during the French Revolution, the democrats treated him no better and he continued to be sent off to foreign lands to die 'for king and country' or for 'le peuple', such as the hapless American 'grunt' conscripted by the inexorable force of modern poverty and sent to Afghanistan, Iraq and all over the world to fight in conflicts he does not understand. There is an added indignity: the taxes that are levied on him, originally for emergencies, but emergencies that for some reason have never gone away and continue to multiply.

Adding insult to injury, the worst indignity the modern age has inflicted on him is to lie to him and tell him that he is now free, the master of his own destiny and the decider of the political direction of his nation.

In comparatively recent history something decisive happened. The financial order had endebted kings, aristocrats and nations beyond their abilities to repay, and yet finance must always grow, must always find new debtors. Thus it turned to Everyman in its hour of need. For that, bankers needed some changes. Everyman had always been cautious and conservative about his expenditure; he had to because of the penury he had hitherto known. Finance needed him to become a debtor and so needed a change of attitude. That change was manufactured by a man called Edward Bernais, a nephew of Sigmund Freud.

Bernais had been one of the architects of the propaganda used to justify the American entrance into the First World War. He was directed by Woodrow Wilson to reassure the world that America was not coming to restore the Ancien Régime, a term used to indicate the old order of monarchy and aristocracy, but to bring 'freedom'. This cynical message worked superbly well.

Bernais was so impressed with the power of his own propaganda that he decided to pursue it in peacetime, but branding it as 'public relations'. Among his many decisive contributions was to transform Everyman's purchasing. Previously man bought what he needed, but people had now to be persuaded to buy what they desired and in the new democratic age, the masses desired some measure of what had previously been the lot of monarchs and aristocrats. Because their incomes had not grown to encompass their desires, people needed the help of their friendly bankers. Thus the masses were enrolled for the next quantum leap in the growth of banking.

What is ignored in this transformation of Everyman into consumer is that a fundamental change in worldview was needed. For man to consume what he desires, he must come to believe existence is based on consumption. In other words, he must believe that man is still an animal that devours. Popular Darwinism, which supplied the final nail in the coffin of Christianity, was used for this transformation. The fatal flaw, however, lies in the fact that, once someone accepts that the nature of existence is consumption, they have implicitly accepted that they too can be consumed. Modern man and woman go out into the world selling themselves as items for consumption, hoping in that trade to acquire the items they wish to consume. They are consumer-consumed.

The money powers were not content even with that, since contentment is not in their nature. Their eternal problem is the exponential growth of their wealth and the exponentially growing need for interest payments, all of which is fuelled by their anxiety, fear of provision and greed. Nothing less than the spread of consumerism around the globe is needed. Most importantly, they need the Muslims to embrace this view of existence since the Muslims are almost a quarter of humanity.

The Muslims are the last deep source of 'Everyman', who, in Arabic, is usually known as 'Zayd'. Zayd still believes in thrift, industry and staying away from usury, because the ayats of the Qur'an and the prophetic hadith are unequivocal about that, and all Muslims know it.

As usual, a Trojan Horse was needed, and this is called Islamic finance and Islamic banking. Although in the siege of Troy, Greeks manned the Horse, the troops manning the Horse today are Trojans, disloyal and treacherous ones. They are Muslims.

The Prophet Muhammad, peace be upon him, said words which can be translated as:

> "Woe to my community from evil scholars ('ulama' as-su') who take this knowledge as a business that they sell to the people in command in their time at a profit for themselves, may Allah not give any profit to their trade." (Al-Hakim in his **History**, from Anas)

When we realise that the people who are in command, in the west and the east, are not the political class but bankers, financiers and corporatists, then it becomes clear who the evil scholars of today are: they are the scholars of Islamic finance and banking.

A recent study of the scholars who are working in the field of so-called 'Islamic Finance' has shown:

> "There are over 400 sharia scholars (sic) worldwide but only around 15 to 20 prominent and experienced ones, which creates demand for scholars to sit on multiple boards. The top 20 scholars hold 14 to 85 positions each, occupying a total of around 620 board positions or 55 percent of the industry."
> "And this leads to sky-high fees paid to the top scholars. A senior banker at an Islamic lender said some scholars could be paid $1,000 to $1,500 per hour of consultation — in addition to an annual bonus of between $10,000 and $20,000 per board seat." (Funds@Work, cited by Reuters)

We do not object to this simply because of the scale of the sums of money involved but because of the principle, for, if the wolf pays the shepherd, what hope have the sheep?

Islamic banking and Islamic finance, which are merely the means that super-banking entities and corporations use to gain access to the wealth of the Muslims, have been expedited by scholars who help them in this process. Now they are serving mega-entities such as HSBC and Goldman Sachs who are determined to plunder Islam and its people as they have plundered the world. Certainly such scholars deserve the name 'evil scholars'. And the scholars who sit quietly by and say nothing are also guilty by endorsing this criminal activity with their silence. And those who are active in establishing halal and wholesome means of commerce for people are heroic.

The means by which these scholars justified this sleight of hand are both extraordinarily complex but surprisingly simple.

Skirting the shari'a

Everyone agrees that if two parties A and B make a contract such that if B will purchase a house A will buy it from him, paying instalments that add up to more than the price of the house, then this is completely forbidden. This is called two sales in one sale and is forbidden by the Prophet, peace be upon him.

> Abu Hurayra narrated that the Prophet, peace be upon him, forbade two sales in one sale. (At-Tirmidhi)

Imam Malik explained one example of this very general prohibition in this way:

> ...a man said to another, "Buy this camel for me with cash so that I can buy it from you on credit." 'Abdullah ibn 'Umar was asked about that and he disapproved of it and forbade it. (Al-Muwatta)

This last explanation is something about which all of the people of knowledge agree, without any dissenting voices. It is a consensus.

But in essence that is what an Islamic bank does. The customer says to the bank, "I want to buy such-and-such a house or car. If you buy it for me, I will enter into an agreement with you to purchase it over a period of years." Everyone agrees that such a contract is utterly forbidden. In reality, the contract is more complicated because the purchaser will partially buy and rent the property but the extra complication is not the issue here.

Islamic banks found an ingenious way to skirt this prohibition. They do not make such a contract, but the purchaser makes a binding promise that he will purchase the house if the bank buys it. This binding promise is written separately, as if nothing to do with the contract, since everyone agrees that such a contract is not allowed. This is, however, clearly just an elaborate means of getting around the prohibition. The reality is that all of the different parts of this agreement, including the separate promise by the purchaser, are in reality one single contract and are thus forbidden.

'Islamic prostitution'

A devastating consequence of this approach is that it can also be applied to prostitution. A man can make a marriage contract with a woman, paying her a dowry, but he can make a separate promise that he will 'divorce' her after an hour. Thus in effect, he has paid her a sum of money to have sexual intercourse with her.

The most charitable interpretation of the role of scholars in Islamic banking is that they have actually held to an important principle: they are trying not to make things difficult for the Muslims. This is an honourable intention.

There is an underlying prior philosophical choice: either we are here to fit in with the existing order of society or we are here as heirs of the prophets to establish the worship of Allah in all aspects of our lives. Most of the work on Islamic finance has been predicated on the assumption that we must simply fit in. This choice has regrettably been strengthened by the barbarities of some of those people who make the other choice, the jihadists. Because of jihadists' 'extremism', other Muslims have chosen to be 'moderates'. But it is a polarisation that is unnecessary. The Muslims have always been engaged in establishing Islam in their particular circumstances and that has always meant taking cognisance of those circumstances. It has always been a middle way.

Yes, the assimilation of Islam to the demands of the present era that Islamic banking represents is only the tip of the iceberg. Regrettably, after decades and more of festering, the disease of consumerism is so far advanced among Muslims that, in an almost emblematic fashion, Makka and Madina have been transformed into gross pastiches of consumer idolatry, shopping paradises with the Hajj and 'Umra pilgrimages mere holiday appendages. That the transformation is tacky and tasteless is perhaps the grossest insult.

In previous times, when Muslims went for the world, they went for the best, but this obscene behaviour has transformed the Noble Cities into horrible caricatures of Batman's Gotham City. Anywhere they occur, such things are offensive to vertebrates — creatures with spines — but to have done such a thing in the two Sacred Mosques is unendurable. The only thing worse than it is the silence of those who should know better — the world Muslim community and its people of knowledge.

It would be all too easy to off-load the blame on to the Saudi regime who are without doubt directly responsible for it. But it cannot be that what is happening at the focal point of all of the Muslims is accidental, particularly not when the Muslims acquiesce in it. That must represent something that has happened to the whole world community. Zayd has joined Everyman as a consumer.

Yet it is precisely in Zayd and Everyman that there lies some hope. For, in spite of everything, Zayd and Everyman still do things because they believe they are the right things to do. Zayd and Everyman are already waking up to the deception that has been perpetrated on them. That has huge implications because the world order has been built on their acquiescence. As the world spirals ever deeper into chaos, politically, socially, intellectually and economically, many ordinary people are questioning the direction our globalised society is taking.

Mutuals

Some of the options open to Zayd and Everyman have already been used by both of them from time immemorial. In the west, these took the form of Mutuals, an example of which were the British 'Friendly Societies', non-profitable organisations that in essence consisted of large numbers of ordinary people putting their funds into a common pool for individuals to withdraw substantial loans from for a variety of purposes.

This practice was widespread among the Muslims, often organised by guilds on behalf of their members and usually associated with a waqf-endowment. As direct competition for banks and the state, these bodies have been sidelined. Yet there is still real potential in such approaches, which will necessarily need work in detaching them from the spurious money whose inflation will otherwise destroy them.

Conclusion

This brief book has omitted far more than it has included. It has not dealt with a huge number of issues. Nor are things referenced in a scholarly way. Much remains for you to do: you the reader, the scholar, the active person and the person who handles money every day.

That money is not the root of all evil is clear. That it has a very significant part in a great deal of evil is hard to overlook. That its evil is because of the warped nature of the money we use and the usurious system that has grown up around it has become obvious, I hope, in this book.

Perhaps nothing will be as significant as simply waking up to an astonishing fact: quite arbitrarily we exchange bits of paper with numbers written on them for things of actual value. We receive bits of paper for the valuable hours of our life in payment for work. We take them and buy the things we need. Worse than that is that we have empowered a group of people to print bits of paper with numbers on them and then spend them as they wish, and to lend them to us at interest. That, of course, is an anachronism. We hardly use paper. Rather we exchange pure abstract numbers using credit and debit cards and on-line banking.

Yet, everything continues because it seems to work, except for temporary blips such as bank runs and crashes, which are all too regular but which we have come to think of as natural phenomena like the weather. All the while, the value of the bits of paper and the digits simply drops, ceaselessly, and sometimes plummets dramatically.

In his novel **The Black Obelisk**, Erich Maria Remarque tells the story of the galloping inflation in Germany between the world wars. People who were lucky enough to have jobs were paid twice a day and would rush out to spend their pay before it dropped in value.

That drama is eclipsed by the more insidious story of the centuries-long drop in value our currencies have suffered. This is well illustrated by William Cobbett, the 19th century activist, who tells us in his **History of the Protestant Reformation** about an Act of Parliament in the time of Henry VIII which set the price of meat. It says: "no person shall take for beef or pork above a half-penny, and for mutton or veal above three-farthings a pound...."[1]

Even middle-aged people can now bore younger people with personal anecdotes of the staggering drop in the value of money. What was slow, centuries-long inflation has now hit the steep part of the exponential curve.

But another type of money has suffered no inflation at all throughout those centuries.

This is a hadith from **Sahih al-Bukhari**:

'Urwa [ibn al-Ja'd] narrated that the Prophet, peace be upon him, gave him a dinar with which to buy a sheep for him. So he bought two sheep with it and sold one of them for a dinar and then brought the sheep and the dinar. Then he [the Prophet, peace be upon him] made a supplication for blessing for him in his trade. He became someone who, even if he had bought dust, he would have made a profit on it.

That dinar would ordinarily buy a sheep, but a good trader was able

1   William Cobbett, History of the Protestant Reformation in England and Ireland; showing how that event has impoverished the main body of the people in those countries, in a series of letters addressed to all sensible and just Englishmen, Letter XVI., No. 454.

to buy two. In this case, he then sold one of the sheep in another market for a dinar. Today, all over the world almost anyone can buy a sheep for the value of that same dinar. Sometimes they can buy two.

That said, we are in a world of shadows and mirrors. Gold, silver and currencies are themselves regarded as saleable items. People buy and sell them. They engage in all sorts of nefarious practices which are too complex for this book. Indeed, governments and international bodies have made the world a playground for these people. The result is that we see prices of ordinary things behaving in ways we do not understand. It seems that in some cases, such as our most basic necessities, they are inexorably going up and up. In other cases prices sometimes plummet, such as gold and silver and the currencies of nations.

Thus, we cannot be simplistic. The modern world is complicated and sophisticated. A one-size-fits-all approach will not work. Therefore let us delineate the outlines of a range of matters to be addressed.

We are inevitably moving beyond the limits we set ourselves in naming this book. So we can only outline what remains to be explored and leave that for another time.

We ought to look at the arena in which money is exchanged for goods, the area that in general we call the 'market'. Clearly we ought to try and understand what relationship there is between what the media call 'the market' or 'market forces' and that other more homely image we have of cattle markets, vegetable markets, and church fairs. The modern market is reserved for high-stakes gamblers. The market laid out with stalls is the domain of the forlorn. From that the question arises: what kind of real market could there be in which the world's commerce of basic necessities could take place and which would give everyone access to it without prohibitive barriers to entering it and without punitive taxation on it? In other words, without barriers at all except prohibition of immoral trade practices and without taxation at all.

We ought also to look at the contractual forms used in buying, selling, hiring, renting, employing, lending, borrowing, partnering and investing. In particular, we have had our curiosity aroused about the inequitable patterns that we have called 'usury' that involve one party taking more than his fair share. That would naturally lead us to investigate possible equitable patterns as well as others that appear to be equitable but are not. Islamic banks and Islamic finance are clear examples of the latter. Given that we could discover all of that, and it is much closer to hand than we anticipated, the question would then be: how has it been lost and how can it be restored? Why did government fall down on its job of preserving justice in the society and in the market? Economic justice is one of the most fundamental types of justice.

But more than anything we should investigate the two entirely different dynamics of 'taking' and 'giving'. These two reach an equilibrium in a just transaction, since when someone gives, someone else takes. But these scales are out of balance and we have a culture of taking. We have reached the extreme condition in which wealth is taken from the poor and needy, by a thousand different taxes and usurious imposts, for the sake of the hyper-wealthy.

Ironically, the cure for the culture of taking is also an act of taking: when the leader of a community takes the zakat from the wealthy of his community and gives it to the eight categories eligible to receive it. It is an act of taking, but from the wealthy and prosperous for the sake of the poor and needy. That is the first step towards another relationship with money.

Islam and the West
The unfortunate impression can have been created that I am positing an ideal 'Islamic' civilisation against a corrupt, usury-ridden Western culture, i.e. a clash of civilisations.

Understanding Islamic civilisation needs the recognition of a number of quite important points. First, it was always composed of Muslims,

Christians, Jews, Zoroastrians, Buddhists and Hindus. They were all accorded the status of 'People of the Book' although details of the rulings are different in various cases. Muslim civilisation was intrinsically multi-ethnic and multi-confessional.

The cornerstone of the Muslim polity is the appointment of a leader for the community. He does not necessarily have to be a global leader. Indeed, this obligation is still the case even if it is only carried out by small communities in a limited fashion. This man is properly the Imam, a term I hesitate to use because of its endless misuse in a variety of ways. He in turn delegates some of his most important functions.

First, he delegates imams to lead the prayers and to deliver the khutbas, assuming of course the existence of mosques for the prayers. The leadership of the prayer and the delivery of the khutba address on Friday are among his most important functions as leader, but since the earliest days that has been delegated to others.

Second, the Prophet, may Allah bless him and grant him peace, established a market at the same time as he established the mosque. Any Muslim leader must make a market place for people, whether that is an open space or a covered space. It has rules. No one can reserve a place in it. No one may be barred from it except for contravention of its fundamental rules. No charge or taxes may be levied on Muslims trading in it, except if needed for maintenance of the market itself.

Third, another of the ruler's primordial tasks is to act as a judge in his community. He is the **Hakim**, which means both ruler and judge. The leader delegates that task by the appointment of qadis — judges — to apply the law when there is contravention of major limiting laws of Islam. In reality, their main function is to adjudicate between people when civil and commercial disputes arise.

The qadi in turn delegates some of his responsibility to the **muhtasib**. This is the man who, among other things, regulates markets. He has to make sure that they are free of usury, that the weights and measures are in order and prevent other types of injustice from taking place.

Another primordial task of the ruler is to ensure that people have a sound currency for their transactions. This book, if it has achieved nothing else, should have given us some hint of the importance of that function. The custom has been widely established for almost two and a half millennia in a wide variety of civilisations that the ruler does that by minting gold and silver coins. He delegates this to the qadi who in turn delegates it to the master of the mint. His role in that is not to make gold and silver available. Rather he must set up a process whereby gold and silver can be assayed to ascertain their purity and then minted with specific purities and weights. The name of the ruler is then included on the coin, as I mentioned earlier. People can bring unminted gold and silver to the mint, or indeed coinage from other countries, and, for a small charge, have them minted anew.

The leader is responsible for da'wa — inviting non-Muslims to Islam. This is both within his domains and without. He is also responsible for the maintenance of jihad and all the external relations of diplomacy or warfare with neighbouring polities. I mention this here without embarrassment. Clearly I am not talking about outlaws waging guerrilla warfare or lone suicide bombers. Rather this is about the leader of a polity doing what the leaders of polities have always done throughout history and continue to do.

This is not the entirety of his duties but a very substantial part of the most important ones.

Muslims are in the position they are in today not merely because of non-Muslim skulduggery but also because of internal failings, very particularly in the commercial zone. For a variety of reasons, the teaching of commercial practice and ordinary transactions was weakened in many Muslim polities. When non-Muslims came with usurious modalities they not only did not reject them but, on the contrary, embraced them. That has been called 'modernism', the slavish desire to emulate non-Muslim behaviour and practice because it is perceived as 'modern'.

On the other side of the equation, among the many competing threads in European and Western history, there is a very discernible one that is reaching out to Islam. Sometimes this is even the case when the people reaching out have not themselves identified that it is Islam they are reaching out towards.

One of the most striking instances of this is directly related to the topic of this book. It is the urgency with which many non-Muslims have been searching for some form of alternative to the usurious financial system. For example, there are many people exploring alternative currencies and investigating the role of gold and silver. That is most starkly contrasted with the corresponding urgency with which many Muslims are still intent on embracing banking, whether personally, in their business lives or as nation-states, in spite of the prohibition of usury and in spite of escalating financial crises.

This is the striking and contrasting picture which presents itself to us today. No one really knows the outcome in the West or in Muslim majority countries. We can say with some conviction that what we have outlined is civilised and that a people who take on these matters can really lay claim to being a civilisation. Conversely whoever opposes them will in the end be the enemy of civilisation. There cannot be a clash of civilisations since there is only civilisation or barbarity.

Postscript

It is sometimes only when things are finished that the beginning is discerned. Allah says that which means, **"So when you have finished, work on, and make your Lord your goal!"** (Surat al-Inshirah 94:7-8)

When one holds a gold or silver coin in one's hand, the need for the argument against fiat money vanishes of itself. With it goes an entire set of prejudices, the first of which is that wealth is intrinsically evil. That is the twin sister of the prejudice that power corrupts and absolute power corrupts absolutely. Both of these mean-spirited attitudes are against life. As Nietzsche said about the 'culture of the Moors of Spain', "... it had to thank noble and manly instincts for its origin... it said yes to life".

The age before us will see the return to the real estimation of wealth as a noble virtue. People may rightly aspire to wealth. But the prior task before us is a complete re-evaluation of the nature of wealth and poverty. How could that not be so? We have already shown the deceptive nature of wealth today.

Moreover, there is another approach via the core meanings of Arabic. The Arabic terms **ghani** and **faqeer** are ordinarily translated as **rich** and **poor**. They really mean **free of need** and **needy** respectively. And as he, peace be upon him, said, "True freedom from need is the heart's freedom from need". That means "true wealth is the heart's wealth".

The Companion az-Zubayr died in battle without leaving a single dinar or dirham for his dependents. Indeed he left an estate encumbered with substantial debt. After four years, his son 'Abdullah finally repaid creditors and came to distribute the money the estate had realised. Each of az-Zubayr's wives received a million and two hundred thousand dirhams. The entire estate was fifty million and two hundred thousand. Thus this wealthy man nevertheless lived sharing the penury of the very poor. The poor, for their part, have often lived as if the wealthiest of Allah's creation since their hearts are content with their lot, as long as it does not descend into utter penury. There is a huge difference between poverty and misery. Muslims may be, and often are, poor, but they are not miserable.

The Messenger of Allah, peace be upon him, was the living proof of that. His personal custom, which he did not require the Muslims to follow, was to empty his house of gold and silver coins each night. If night descended before he had done that, then he would wait while Bilal found suitable recipients for them. Thus, he started every day entirely anew, trusting in Allah.

Further reading and viewing

Imam Malik ibn Anas, **al-Muwatta**, Diwan Press. The earliest and most authentic source on the behaviour of the first three generations of Islam and of the Messenger of Allah, may Allah bless him and grant him peace. It contains the fullest account of how those generations transacted in the market-place and in buying and selling generally.

Shaykh Dr. Abdalqadir as-Sufi, **The Return of the Khalifate,** in which the author shows the hand international finance and banking had in the demise of the Osmanli khalifate and the logical corollary, the route to its revival.

Banking: The Root Cause of the Injustices of Our Time, Diwan Press. These are the transcripts of a Norwich seminar from 1987 given by a group of Muslims on the nature of usury and the effect that it has had on our society. The material was updated and republished in 2009. There is a revealing paper on two non-usurious societies – Renaissance Venice and the Ottoman Empire. It is a useful general introduction to the subject of usury. It has been updated with an account of the foundation of the Federal Reserve and an essay outlining a return to the Sunna of Islamic trading.

William Cobbett, **A History of the Protestant Reformation**, James Duffy and Co., Ltd., Dublin. Cobbett researched all the original sources such as the Acts of Parliament which inaugurated the usurious banking age in Britain. From there he traces the causes of the American Declaration of Independence and the French Revolution.

William Cobbett, **Paper Against Gold**, Diwan Press. To be published by Diwan Press in 2015. Cobbett's analysis of the nature of paper money and gold.

"Nasa-funded study: industrial civilisation headed for 'irreversible collapse'?" cited by Nafeez Ahmed in the Guardian: http://www.theguardian.com/environment/earth-insight/2014/mar/14/nasa-civilisation-irreversible-collapse-study-scientists

Video
An excellent series called **The Medici, Godfathers of the Renaissance** based on a book of the same name by Strathern on the famed Italian banking dynasty. It is far more than a story of banking for it shows how it in turn lies at the root of the Renaissance, the Reformation, humanism, the scientific revolution and thus the modern world.

The Corporation is a Canadian documentary film written by Joel Bakan, and directed by Mark Achbar and Jennifer Abbott. The documentary examines the modern-day corporation, considering its legal status as a class of person and evaluating its behaviour towards society and the world at large as a psychiatrist might evaluate an ordinary person. This is explored through specific examples. Bakan wrote the book, **The Corporation: The Pathological Pursuit of Profit and Power,** during the filming of the documentary.

Concursante, Rodrigo Cortés' 2007 Spanish language film which, through the story of a man who wins the biggest prize ever in a TV competition, tells eloquently of the deception in modern monetarism, finance and banking.

Money as Debt, Paul Grignon's 47-minute animated presentation tells in simple and effective graphic terms what money is and how it is being created. (http://tinyurl.com/ctdsyn)

Margrit Kennedy speaks on interest free economy: https://www.youtube.com/watch?v=QuBy3BzCXwg

A Balkan Tale (http://www.balkantale.com/videos.php) on the decline of the Osmanlı commonwealth and the appalling rise of the nation-statism that was to rend its fabric so devastatingly.

Milton Keynes UK
Ingram Content Group UK Ltd.
UKHW050913261124
451529UK00022B/623